ORGANIZATION AND MANAGEMENT

LONDON : GEOFFREY CUMBERLEGE
OXFORD UNIVERSITY PRESS

Organization and Management

SELECTED PAPERS

BY

CHESTER I. BARNARD

PRESIDENT, NEW JERSEY BELL TELEPHONE COMPANY

HARVARD UNIVERSITY PRESS

Cambridge, Massachusetts

1948

PRINTED IN THE UNITED STATES OF AMERICA

PREFACE

FOR many years I have been practicing the arts of organizing and managing in widely divergent types of organizations. This experience has increasingly generated a curiosity of a scientific kind concerning the nature of organizations and the means of determining the behavior of those whose activities compose them. This has led to a number of papers and lectures about various aspects of organization and of the practice of management.

One integrated set of these papers, a course of Lowell Institute Lectures given in 1937, was converted into book form in *The Functions of the Executive*.[1] A few have appeared first in book symposiums of papers by several authors; still others were first published in journals. Some of the more important, however, were printed privately and were distributed only to my friends and associates in business, public affairs, and academic life, and have not been available to the public.

The generous reception of *The Functions of the Executive* and the frequent requests for copies of reprints of papers have suggested the publication of a collection of them restricted to those that now seem of more permanent value.

The papers selected are presented herein in the order of date of first publication or delivery. Where necessary, an explanatory note concerning the paper is presented with it and, therefore, further comment here seems in most instances unnecessary. However, I should like to make special comment about three of them.

"Concepts of Organization." This is an exegesis of the ap-

[1] Harvard University Press, 1938.

proach to the study of organization as embodied in *The Functions of the Executive*. It is adapted from an article entitled "Comments on the Job of the Executive" which appeared in the *Harvard Business Review* (Spring, 1940). This was a rejoinder to a critique of *The Functions of the Executive* by Professor Morris A. Copeland of the Harvard Graduate School of Business Administration, published in the *Harvard Business Review* (Winter, 1940). Professor Copeland, among other criticisms, questioned the inclusion of the activities of customers as parts of an organization. He also challenged the conceptual scheme I employed and the general theoretical treatment of the subject. In rewriting the answers to these criticisms I have restated the questions raised in general terms as valid questions that might properly be asked by anyone interested, and have eliminated those parts of my reply that were specially applicable to Professor Copeland's personal position.

The latter part of this paper deals with the importance of the theoretical approach to the study of organization and sets forth the conceptual framework I used in writing *The Functions of the Executive*. It needs no further comment here.

The first part of the paper, however, deals with the concept of organization. It is highly abstract and to many seems unrealistic. Indeed, in everyday work, for most purposes I continue to conceive of an organization as constituted of a group of people, usually restricted to those "on the payroll." But for more general and for scientific purposes I became convinced that such a restricted and "practical" concept was inadequate. After nine years of experience with it, it continues, for me, a more convenient and effective intellectual tool than any I know for working with the subject. Indeed, even for practical purposes I found it an extremely useful concept in the work of developing and managing the United Service Organizations, Inc. (USO), during World War II, the most difficult

single organization and management task in my experience.
It puts the emphasis upon organization as coordinated activities
rather than upon the individuals who are the actors. The latter
are often simultaneously "members" of several organizations,
and their activities are not infrequently to be conceived as
simultaneously functions of more than one organization.
Moreover, the relationship of individuals to organization is
frequently so ephemeral that they are not conveniently regarded as "members" of an organization, whereas, in my view,
certain of their activities must clearly be regarded as a part
of the "organized" activities associated with and, as I prefer to
think, constituting organization. This concept of organization is a "field" concept in which activities take place in and
are governed by a field of "forces," some human and social,
some physical. Whether the field approach which others
have deemed useful as respects social phenomena (Cf. J. F.
Brown, *Psychology and the Social Order;* Kurt Lewin, *Principles of Topological Psychology*) will prove in the long run
as useful as the constructs "magnetic field," "electrical field,"
and "gravitational field" in physical science remains to be
determined by experience.

"On Planning for World Government." This was written
for the Conference on Science, Philosophy and Religion (Fall
of 1943), at the request of R. M. MacIver, Harlow Shapley,
Lyman Bryson, and Rabbi Finkelstein, conveyed to me by the
latter. The thought was that too many scholars and scientists
were naïve with respect to the nature and possibilities of
"planning" in the field of human relations and organization.
In other words, I was asked to do a bit of "debunking" of the
exaggerated notions and claims of the "planners" in general
and of those "planning" world government in particular.
Whether or not the effort to this end was successful is not
relevant here. In the attempt I presented new material on
both the structure and the operation of organizations and

especially developed the idea of the autonomic organization of
social activities through the free operation of formal organizations effected through voluntary lateral agreements.

The considerations set forth in contrasting hierarchical and
lateral organizations relate essentially to the main political
problem of our times — the choice between totalitarianism and
free societies. Notwithstanding the slogans of the advocates
of the "free enterprise" system, the bias in the United States is
strongly toward the multiplication of formal organizations and
the integration of them into formal organizations of large
size.[2] We believe more and more in planning and in our

---

[2] Cf. Dr. Margaret Mead: "The Application of Anthropological Techniques
to Cross-National Communication," *Transactions of the New York Academy
of Sciences,* Series II, Vol. 9, No. 4, pp. 133–152, February 1947. At page 141
Dr. Mead says:

"Another sort of misunderstanding which influenced communication was
the difference between the British and American sense of the real world. The
Americans see the world as man-controlled, a vast malleable space on which one
builds what one wishes, from blueprints one has drawn, and, when dissatisfied,
simply tears the structure down and starts anew. The great sense of mechanical
control of the environment — product, at least in part, of an empty continent
and the machine age — extends to American attitudes towards crops and
animals, which are again something to be planned for, streamlined, increased
or decreased at will, and even, to a certain degree, to human beings, who can
be, if not completely molded by man-made devices, at least sorted mechanically
into simply defined pigeonholes. The British, in contrast, see the world as a
natural world to which man adapts himself, in which he assumes no control
over the future but only the experienced foresight of the husbandman or the
gardener, who plants the best seed and watches carefully over the first green
blades. Man is seen as the junior partner of God (expressed in either con-
ventional or more contemporary forms, but still as the junior partner of forces
to which he can adapt himself but which he cannot control). He can 'only
handle one link in the chain of destiny at a time.'"

At first consideration it may seem strange that Americans who preach individualism and free enterprise should in practice behave so much in accordance with the ideology of "planning" and deliberate patterned control whereas
the British proceeding rapidly to State socialism should have an aversion to
the kind of behavior it implies. This kind of contradiction between an ideo-
logical complex and the rationale of concrete behavior is very common in
ethics and morals, politics, and business.

ability by taking thought to construct the large patterns determining our destiny. This is a faith in control of, rather than in essentially unpremeditated global adaptation to, the environment. There is a corresponding decline in faith in the capacity of a system of formally uncontrolled but nevertheless interdependent units to adapt autonomically to the environment. Adam Smith's "unseen hand" seems more and more incredible — and discreditable. Yet, lacking the omniscience required for effective planning to control the environment, we are compelled really to operate on the strategic factors,[3] the single links in the chain, one at a time, though it may be admitted that these single links are often complex systems of "links within links."

We cannot escape the unconscious adaptation of the complex interaction of the innumerable variables of our societies.[4] Indeed, an important technique in the management of large formal organizations is training, conditioning, and selection of personnel such that autonomically, groups as a whole behave appropriately to the conditions without conscious control. This is an implicit aim in much education. Yet the impossibility of escaping autonomic adaptation and the rationale of such adaptation both seem to elude most of us, perhaps because of false intellectual pride or fear of mysticism.[5]

[3] Cf. *The Functions of the Executive,* chapter xiv.

[4] I do not imply, of course, that adaptation is always achieved.

[5] Pareto in *The Mind and Society,* passim, discusses the problem clearly. See also M. Polanyi, "The Growth of Thought in Society," *Economica,* 1941, p. 428; and F. A. v. Hayek, "Scientism and the Study of Society," *Economica,* 1942, p. 267; 1943, p. 34; 1944, p. 27.

Consider also the analogous problem of plan and purpose in modern theories of biological evolution and adaptation. "Adaptation is real, and it is achieved by a progressive and directed process. This process is natural, and it is wholly mechanistic in its operation. This natural process achieves the aspect of purpose, without the intervention of a purposer, and it has produced a vast plan, without the concurrent action of a planner." George Gaylord Simpson: "The Problem of Plan and Purpose in Nature," *Scientific Monthly,* Vol. LXIV, No. 6 (June 1947), p. 495.

Thus we confront repeatedly both an organizational and an intellectual dilemma. In organization we often have to choose whether it is best to manage by explicit direction or to establish general conditions and then "let nature take its course." Intellectually, we have to decide whether deliberately to alter one of the variables of a system, making the false assumption that we know the unknowns, i.e., that "other things remain equal" or fixed or are irrelevant to a new combination; or whether to let blind trial and error evolve until finally perhaps an acceptable solution is attained.[6]

"Functions and Pathology of Status Systems in Formal Organizations." This essay was originally stimulated by certain dogmatic positions taken by C. E. Ayres in his book *The Theory of Economic Progress* (University of North Carolina Press, 1944) to the effect that social status or differences in social status are a maleficent inheritance from the age of mythology. This doctrine stems from Thorstein Veblen — in my view brilliant, stimulating, cynical, iconoclastic — and superficial. On reading Ayres's book at the request of the publisher, for the first time I set myself to the task of considering the functions of status in formal organizations. My reflections on this subject took the form of the present paper as a basis for a lecture at the University of Chicago in August

[6] Somewhat this kind of alternative analogously appears to occur in biological adaptation. Th. Dobzhansky and M. F. Ashley Montagu, in "Natural Selection and the Mental Capacities of Mankind" (*Science,* Vol. 105, No. 2736, June 6, 1947, p. 587), point out that evolutionary adaptation occurs either by (a) genetic fixity where the trait is fixed by heredity and hence appears in the bodily development of the individual regardless of environmental variation; or (b) by way of a genetically controlled plasticity of traits, the ability to respond to a given range of environmental situations by evolving traits favorable in these particular situations. The first, so to speak "planned," type is of benefit to organisms whose milieu remains uniform and static. "Conversely, organisms which inhabit changeable environments are benefitted by having their traits plastic and modified by each recurrent configuration of environmental agents in a way most favorable for the survival of the carrier of the trait in question."

1945. It is worth repeating here what I said to my audience on that occasion: "The most significant thing I have to say is that although I have been studying and talking and writing about organization and management for many years and have also been constantly concerned with practical problems of status, it is not until this late day that I have attained a realization that status is necessarily systematized in formal organizations, and not until now that I have secured an explicit understanding of the functions of status systems. It is a case where the broader aspects of what one knows as a matter of course and of what one applies as a matter of 'know how' may completely escape explicit consideration. The forest is missed because of the proximity of the trees. This is a persistent kind of limitation of those whose knowledge comes from intimate experience though the latter is nevertheless indispensable, I think, to a thorough understanding of organization." I had left out of my book if not Hamlet, perhaps Ophelia, and did not discover it for seven years — and no one reported the omission to me!

In editing these papers for the present publication it has seemed desirable to include additional footnotes. Those added are enclosed in brackets [ ]. Those unbracketed were contained in the original papers.

CHESTER I. BARNARD

South Orange, N. J.,
June 12, 1947.

CONTENTS

CONTENTS

ORGANIZATION AND MANAGEMENT

I

SOME PRINCIPLES AND BASIC CONSIDERATIONS IN PERSONNEL RELATIONS[1]

IT is my purpose to discuss principles and fundamental considerations in personnel relations, rather than concrete practices, policies, or schemes of organization. Much of my effort during the last twenty-five years both in private business and in public work has been spent in these so-called "practical" activities, in the actual management of organizations of large size, so complex as obviously to require a rather bewildering array of plans, schemes, policies, organizations, and the other paraphernalia of modern large scale industrial or governmental undertakings. Yet I am sure that a consideration of general purposes, "principles," and underlying conceptions — what we may call the philosophic approach to the concrete problems — is intensely practical. Indeed, it is almost necessary that we unite in such an approach in order that our consideration of the specific problems may be intelligent, and that our discussion of them may be intelligible. In conferences such as this, our consideration is chiefly of specific plans, methods, and programs, discussed independently and with much attention to internal structure, details, and immediate purposes. The danger is that we shall lose sight of the general problem and forget to formulate the major and ultimate objectives by which all else must be finally tested. Not infrequently our failures in this respect permit us to do well what had best not be done at all, or to do badly or omit what may be essential.

[1] An address to the Fifth Summer Conference Course in Industrial Relations, Graduate College, Princeton University, September 20, 1935. Printed for private distribution in 1935.

The Place of the Individual in Personnel Relations

The first group of remarks I would make in this general approach refers to the place of the individual in industrial relations.

Despite constant reference to the individual and individualism in the political discussion of present day conditions, it seems to be a fact that the conditions of modern life tend to obscure the position of the individual, especially in economic affairs and socially. We still give much lip service to the forgotten individual, but the whole complex of thought, except when our immediate personal concerns are involved, relates to the cooperative and social aspects of life. We are so engrossed constantly with the problems of organization that we neglect the unit of organization and are quite unaware of our neglect. It almost seems to be to our purpose to forget the individual except as he compels consideration.

If I understand what I read of history correctly, this state of mind which so obsesses us has been accumulating for many centuries, and with greatest rapidity in recent times. Neglecting entirely the ancient periods, and beginning about A.D. 600, most of the elements in the progress of civilization have had the effect of minimizing the individual, barring exceptional men, as an essential factor in progress. Man was tied to land, about which developed and overlay a feudal system of rights and obligations. Except as to purely spiritual respects, his relation to the church seems similarly to have been institutionalized. Later, industrial development involved subordination to the guild and the development of national political life, with subordination to the monarch or the nation.

With the American and French Revolutions and the opening of vast pioneer countries, a substantial reversal of the trend developed, as to important sections of the world population, especially in political respects, also evidenced in the movement for universal education. But many new things of the nineteenth century reversed this temporary change in attitude. Of these, the theory of evolution, the emphasis upon the biological background of the individual, and the study of sociology and social anthropology profoundly affected the importance of the individual in our habits of thought. And to these, the study of economics and economic speculation, especially of the French, German and English socialists, gradually contributed enormously. Then finally flowered the modern corporation and the organized labor movement, all emphasizing interdependence, cooperation, regimentation, as the essential aspects of life, as the constructive forces of civilization, until the subservience of individual to state, society, economic machinery, is the habitual attitude of mind. It has become exceedingly difficult to consider the individual. Chiefly the psychologist, the psychiatrist, the physician, the clergyman, and (to some extent) the teacher, recognize "man" as an individual, rather than as a statistical unit, in the major aspects of their work.

I am not making a plea for "individualism" as opposed to "collectivism." The extreme emphasis upon the individual in doctrinaire argument against various aspects of collective interest and action seems to me even less realistic than the reverse emphasis upon organization and collectivism. Not only socially and politically but also economically, men are more interdependent, at least in western civilization, than ever before. By reason of organized cooperation in innumerable ways, both population and the standard of living, and perhaps even the quality of living, have been greatly increased. Without such organization in society, retrogression is inevitable. Recognition of these facts, however, does not require a denial of the coexistence of the individual. It is individuals who are being organized, and the effectiveness of the group depends not only upon the scheme of grouping and function, but upon the quality of the elementary units. It is impossible in practice to disregard either aspect very far; but in general our condition of mind, our attention and interest in the problems of organization, dispose us constantly to a one-sided approach.

This is quite evident in industrial relations. I believe I have seen again and again, in various business and other organizations I have been able closely to observe, that either the wrong thing is done or the right thing done very badly, because of the attempt to find a short cut which fails to take into account the individual as the key to the effective operation of all these plans and schemes of coordination.

In some respects the truth of what I am saying is recognized as a matter of course by both private and public employers. In the selection of employees, for instance, frequently a quite careful consideration and appraisal of the individual is involved. Much expense and effort is expended in this process. Again, in the effort to secure productive efficiency, individual job training has had great development in many industries in the last thirty years. Similarly, in many activities, supervisors are trained and managed to promote their effectiveness in the development of the individual employee. A little reflection will convince that emphasis upon the individual in personnel relations is in complete harmony with the inescapable daily practice of industry. Nevertheless, in connection with general personnel policies, and in the management of the less obvious aspects of supervisory work, the tendency is very strong to neglect the individual employee and to deal exclusively with masses and averages. It is difficult, and sometimes expensive for the short run, to particularize.

My own belief is strong that the capacity, development, and state of mind of employees as individuals must be the focal point of all policy and practice relating to personnel. Why this should be so is well illustrated in Dr. Elton Mayo's recent book *Human Problems of an Industrial Civilization*, in which he describes some experimental personnel research in one of the Western Electric Company plants. A number of different practices affecting working conditions were tried out upon a group of operatives under controlled conditions, to see what the effect would be upon the efficiency of the individual employees. For example, change in lighting conditions, arrangement and order of rest periods, differences in kind and time of lunches, etc., etc. In the course of these experiments remarkable increases in individual production were accomplished. When the experiments were reversed, to see what the results would be under less satisfactory working conditions for the same employees, all were amazed that the falling off in efficiency did not develop. This finally led to a demonstration of the fact that the mental reaction of the employee to the individualized atmosphere (not greater individual supervision in the ordinary sense) was the principal factor rather than the detail of working conditions. The latter were of superficial or intermediate importance. It was learned, in many instances, that home conditions rather than working conditions are the controlling factor — something that any experienced manager can testify to on the basis of the more extreme cases.

We must recognize that the individual employee is a human being, who spends only a part of his time in our plants. For sixteen to twenty years perhaps, his background was entirely outside industry. He is now married, has children, relatives, belongs to clubs, etc. His whole state of mind is a reflection of his past, biologically and socially, of his present physiology and of his environment outside of working hours. His reaction to what his employer says or proposes, to his working conditions, to his employer's attitudes, purposes, and interests, is affected sometimes to a controlling degree, by these conditions entirely outside the scope of the employer's authority or influence. All that the employer can do is to adjust his treatment of the individual employee to the state of mind and the condition of the man as he is.

I will even go so far as to say that on many general policies we should think not of the man but his wife, because she frequently has a more objective understanding of the man and his position in industry than can the employer. It is frequently true that a policy, course of action, or treatment that would be recognized by the women of the family as on the whole sound and fair would be so, or at least if the women could not so regard them, then some modification or adjustment was likely to be in order.

I have hurriedly set before you some of the reasons why I lay so much emphasis upon the individual. In a world that increasingly stresses organization, schemes, policies, mass methods, it is good and practical to have persistently in mind that the key to dynamic effort in all industry is the individual and his willingness to develop in it. This will seem to many as an ideal of remote practical application. It so impressed me when my attention was first actively drawn to such a statement several years ago when the late E. K. Hall, who took such an active interest in these Princeton conferences, undertook to formulate for many of our executives the purposes or objects of the Bell System personnel policy. A part of his statement was to the effect that a major purpose was the development of the individual to the utmost. At that time I subscribed to this statement as an ideal, with many doubts and reservations as to its practical significance or consequence in the everyday work of management. Since then continual observation and the analysis of my own experience in public and private organizations has convinced me that his idealization, if you wish to call it that, of personnel objectives is highly practical in the long view.

A word of caution about it is not superfluous. If this development of the individual is to be a central consideration in all personnel work, it should be so genuinely, not merely as a matter of tactics, nor merely or chiefly a matter of industrial efficiency. It will ultimately fail if it is merely a high sounding fiction for stimulating production and good morale. Hypocrisy is fatal in the management of personnel. I will relate an incident which illustrates what I mean.

A few years ago a brilliant lawyer, one of my friends, thought he ought to tell me that the system of justice encompassed by the law and the courts had the purpose, after all, not of according justice to individuals, but of preserving a system of orderly and peaceful conduct of affairs for society as a whole. Whether this was an original thought or came from Blackstone or Lord Coke or Montesquieu, I do not know; but it is the kind of statement that appeals to the modern mind in justification of systems of procedure and organization which exist ostensibly for the benefit of individuals. As such it pleased my intellectual fancy. But my rejoinder was:

That may be true. Grant that the important and immediate practical consequence of a system of jurisprudence is exactly what you say. Nevertheless, when the time comes, as it would, that the individuals to whom it is to be applied, recognize it only as a system for serving the State, as a method of getting rid of disputes and conflicts but without interest in justice as such, then the power behind that system will dissipate and its manipulators will degenerate into administrators of the expedient.

A major personnel objective that is merely expedient will, I think, in the end prove futile to its sponsors and abortive to those who come within its scope.

THE WILL TO COLLABORATE

I suppose that the primary purpose in the minds of those who develop personnel policies and who manage businesses and organization is generally not to develop individuals but to facilitate the working together of groups of people toward definite ends. In my view this purpose is secondary in point of order but equally important to that of developing the individual, and the two together constitute the entire legitimate purpose of management so far as the personnel is concerned. It is the cooperative aspect of personnel management that has had most attention, disproportionately so. There is a great volume of technics, practices, schemes, plans, organizations, schedules, devices put into practice and necessary to effect this cooperation. Most of it is local or special to particular industries, plants or managements and calls for no discussion at a session of this kind. It all involves, however, one major problem to which I have seldom seen conscious attention given — the willingness, desire, and interest of the individual in cooperative effort. Any such effort requires the ability to function in conjunction with others in specific ways, a technic of operation or production, a management or control or directing agency, and the will to collaborate. This latter aspect is called by various names, such as loyalty, esprit de corps, desire for team play, etc., and is promoted by the various methods, to which much attention has been given in many industries.

Nevertheless, a critical examination would reveal that the weakest link in the chain of cooperative effort is the will to collaborate. In point of fact, I think it is true, though we are loath to admit it, that our hands are held back again and again in doing things known to be technically or commercially feasible, because of the fear that the human beings with whom we work will not sufficiently collaborate with us or with each other. This is especially true where a change of customary practice may be involved, or where the advantages are not immediate or are indefinite so far at least as workers are concerned. In work-a-day parlance this is expressed by such phrases as "Well, you can't get away with that" or "Your people won't go along with that" or "They won't work together on that" or "There will be friction that we can't handle or control." These are typical expressions of the fact that in all organized groups, industrial, political or social, there are serious limitations in the development of the will to collaborate. Though we like to take pride in the accomplishments of organized effort, we are frequently only able to do so by leaving out of sight the possibilities of accomplishment if we knew how to get people better to work together wholeheartedly for common purposes only remotely related to individual purposes.

The reasons for our limited accomplishments may be many; but the vital one is lack of confidence in the sincerity and integrity of management. It is the lack of that confidence, rather than defects of technic or competence, which insidiously thwarts the best efforts that are made in the industrial world. It is the recognition of that lack of confidence that discourages the most promising developments. And so the advancement of the interests of all is retarded.

In the long run I know of only one way to obtain confidence and that is to deserve it. At root, the matter is one only of plain honesty. It is unnecessary to expatiate on that subject. When a condition of honesty and sincerity is recognized to exist, errors of judgment, defects of ability, are sympathetically endured. They are expected. Employees don't ascribe infallibility to leaders or management. What does disturb them is insincerity and the appearance of insincerity when the facts are not in their possession.

This appearance of insincerity is unfortunately allowed to develop by essentially honest and sincere men, by a strange trait of human nature — the love of smart tricks. A "flyer" in short cuts, a gamble on "getting away with" unsound or dishonest tactics seems to entice men of honest and sound purpose, just as the desire to take chances induces men to occasional gambles in financial matters, contrary to their judgment and principles. I know of nothing more difficult to check in a management organization of tried, experienced men of integrity and of fine purpose in personnel relations than this sporadic propensity to be smart, to avoid an issue, to withhold an unpleasant truth, to decline to admit an error, when honesty, sincerity, and even good sense clearly condemn such lapses. There is not much hope that men can be invariably so self-controlled as always to avoid these things; but they ought to be discouraged. When they are discouraged, when the main and continuing purpose is sincere and honest, these incidents are not fatal. Employees no more expect individual moral perfection than they do infallibility.

Perhaps some will think that again I am voicing an impracticable ideal in personnel relations, especially those who think they observe in the real world of industrial relations little evidence of honesty and sincerity. It is not so. Many large and innumerable small employers operate essentially on this basis as a matter of course. Many may believe that employees do not respond to fair and honest management. I am convinced to the contrary. The test of the correctness of this view is best obtained under adverse circumstances. I have myself seen large groups of employees voluntarily and wholeheartedly cooperate to increase individual and collective efficiency and production in order to reduce expenses when it was recognized that the immediate effect was to the pecuniary disadvantage of the employees themselves. The importance of such collaboration to all involved is incalculable. It is neither justified, nor can it be obtained, except on the basis of a confidence inspired by experience. The respect of an organization or of a management can be acquired only as is that of the individual — not by what he says today or said yesterday but by both word and deed through a succession of many days.

Welfare Plans in Personnel Relations

In the last thirty-five years industrial practice has developed greatly in the adoption of plans for the welfare of employees, theretofore considered inappropriate or not feasible. Accident compensation practice, sickness benefits, medical protection, pensions, accident prevention, recreation facilities, are the more important and generally used, but there are many others less generally employed which in the aggregate represent a substantial contribution to the welfare of employees. Not least of them are the greatly improved working conditions, especially as to light, air, temperature, cleanliness, etc. As a whole these special practices are regarded as essentially for the benefit of employees and as constituting the main features of improved personnel relations.

These special plans have been adopted from a variety of motives, depending upon the management and circumstances. That they do improve personnel relations, other things equal, that they increase interest and loyalty to work or service if not to the employer, that they on the whole improve efficiency and promote morale and cooperative attitudes is undoubtedly true. Many of them within restricted limits are commendable and justified from many points of view. But they are not a substitute for a positive management of personnel, and they will not in themselves do much to develop the individual or to foster the will to collaborate — the two essential aims, as I see it, of sound personnel policy. As a substitute for the proper conduct of employee relations they are futile and dangerous. They tend to create in the minds of management a presumption of fair and constructive relations with employees when in fact they may represent merely a philanthropic attitude or an attempt to "buy off" hostile states of mind. It is clear in my mind that philanthropy, as such, has no legitimate place in industrial relations, and that the idea of buying good relations is abortive. The very notion creates a state of mind on the part of management that will blind it to the essential problems. Hence, such welfare plans and activities, though they have an important place in the proper conduct of business and may be sound adjuncts to the right kind of personnel relations, are not in my opinion an important aspect of the fundamental problems of industrial relations. They are details. I only mention them here because the tendency is sometimes strong to regard them as the central feature of personnel work.

The limits to welfare plans are therefore much narrower in my view than with those who advocate them for what may be called ulterior motives. In their minds the limits will be set theoretically by what can be spent in view of the anticipated business benefits; whereas I think it sound to carry on these activities only to the extent that their cost is not a substantial proportion of the payroll, and the benefits are substantial as compared with other methods reasonably available to the employee. In other words the element of paternalism should be at a minimum, and welfare schemes should not be considered a substitute for wages.

Economic Motives in Personnel Relations

The best accomplishments in personnel relations require something more than emphasis upon first principles and ethics, or the assignment of welfare activities to their proper place. It is equally necessary to correct false ideas regarding business and its conduct, which prevent an understanding of personnel problems and their solution.

It is an almost universal assumption that managers and owners in the detailed conduct of business are governed almost completely or exclusively by purely economic motives. Business men are inclined to insist that this is true and would appear usually to be ashamed to admit that it is not true in their individual cases.

In the broad sense that no business can escape its balance sheet, it is true that the economic or money motive governs the administration of business. Nevertheless my observation in several different well-managed businesses convinces me that business decisions are constantly being made that are not based upon economic motives. This is something that business men seldom admit, and of which they are frequently unaware. Prestige, competitive reputation, social philosophy, social standing, philanthropic interests, combativeness, love of intrigue, dislike of friction, technical interest, Napoleonic dreams, love of accomplishing useful things, desire for regard of employees, love of publicity, fear of publicity — a long catalogue of noneconomic motives actually condition the management of business, and nothing but the balance sheet keeps these noneconomic motives from running wild. Yet without all these incentives I think most business would be a lifeless failure. There is not enough vitality in dollars to keep business running on any such scale as we experience it, nor are the things which can be directly purchased with money an adequate incentive.

The business man can't admit this. He seems to think he would lose caste. He feels it necessary to take a "hard-boiled" attitude. He must do everything efficiently and "not the way politicians do them." Or he fears the bankers might think him soft. (I have found them just like the rest of us but they won't admit it either.) Part of this is professional pose. Some of it is the reaction to the unpleasant things that responsibility imposes — a sort of self-protective psychology. But if you will stop taking the business man at his word and quietly watch him when he is off guard, you will find he is taking care of poor old John who couldn't be placed anywhere else, that he is risking both profit and failure rather than cut wages, that he continues an unprofitable venture on nothing but hope rather than throw his men out of work. Much of this is unsound. It would be better if economic motives did operate more effectively, but the point is that it is impossible to get to the root of personnel relations or understand labor troubles or successes on the unrealistic assumption that economic motives exclusively govern. They merely limit and guide. They control more in some cases or some businesses than others.

An equally fallacious assumption is that economic motives are those which chiefly govern the attitude of employees to business and management. Employees frequently indicate that money is all they work for or are interested in, so far as employment goes. It is not true. Any manager knows better. Most employees know better. I will not take the time to catalogue the motives of employment and the tragic deficiency of motives which it is one of the functions of personnel management to correct. But there can be no understanding of the personnel problem if it is assumed that wages can buy peace or satisfaction.

A third disturbing false assumption is that the economic motive operating in business is a profit motive. Though the hope of profit is the mainspring of industrial enterprise and therefore of industrial employment, it is not the dominating economic motive in the conduct of going business. Fear of loss, not profit, dominates the business complex. This fear is not peculiar to businesses organized for profit, but inheres equally in enterprises of a non-profit character, such as hospitals, philanthropic foundations, government departments, etc. As a practical force affecting personnel relations in all kinds of employment, industrial or otherwise, I should think effort to prevent loss is many times as important as the effort to secure profit. If this is true, it is exceedingly important to recognize it, because it is easily demonstrated that all interests coincide on the question of losses. Men cannot be paid, they cannot even be employed, if outgo exceeds income.

Now I am attempting to advocate neither an economic nor a social theory. It is not necessary to accept my opinion as to the degree to which economic motives or the profit motive does or does not operate in business or employment — I submit that to a substantial and significant degree it is not true that economic motives do or can dominate industrial relations, and that this is especially true of the profit motive. Though almost everywhere, from all sources, a contrary opinion is expressed or implied, I believe I have related facts that are very generally known or can be readily observed and that are almost necessary by the logic of industrial conditions. The point is that a proper understanding of labor problems or the development of correct and effective industrial relations policy must be based upon the actual conditions, not upon fictions.

BARGAINING VS. COOPERATION

Most of the people who talk about "labor," and ostensibly on its behalf, seem to know very little about the actual problems of day by day personnel work. They seem to know a good deal about social conditions and about some of the diseases of industrialism, but little of its physiology. They would, I fear, not understand my conception of the purposes or methods of industrial relations. Moreover, they evidently have a conception of the processes and motives of business conduct that seems false to me, and a view of the employee that also does not agree with my knowledge. It is not surprising, therefore, that their proposals for the improvement of industrial relations should seem wrong from my point of view. At any rate, their solution is "collective bargaining," and they therefore endeavor not merely to make collective bargaining possible, but to make it the only orthodox practice in industrial relations. Hence, Section 7-A of the National Industrial Recovery Act and the recent Wagner Labor Act.

There are many men in this hall representing institutions that have progressed far beyond the philosophy of bargaining, and they recognize that these achievements are endangered not by the Act, but by the philosophy, the habit of thought, the moral attitude that is inherent in it. These institutions believed, and their employees believed, that they had secured progress in labor relations beyond any that had been attained in history, and can only regard it as deplorable that those who advocate or endorse this legislation do not, cannot, or will not recognize it.

Stripped of the politics, strategic attitudes, and misinformation which clothe this subject, the issue is whether "bargaining" can or does permit the promotion of the welfare of employees and industrial harmony, or whether cooperation is the process by which these ends can be attained. It is apparently not recognized that in industrial relations bargaining generally precludes a cooperative state of mind; and it is assumed that "cooperation" is merely a cover for a completely one-sided state of affairs. Underlying the attitudes that are expressed in these opposed views of industrial relation, I think lie opposed economic and social conceptions.

Some "Collective Bargainers" appear to consider that there exists a marginal fund in industrial operations out of which either higher wages and improved working conditions or profits can be taken, and that the problem is one of distribution of this fund, essentially to be determined by the strategy and power of two opposed groups — employees and employers. The "collective cooperationers," on the other hand, do not believe that there is such a fund in general, and that therefore the improvement of employees' conditions can only come from the increased effectiveness of employment, the result of which must accrue either through wages and associated conditions or through prices, or both, with profits, if there are any in the aggregate, being the same.

Other "collective bargainers" apparently subscribe to a "cost plus" theory of making prices, and this underlies the attitude regarding bargaining. They assume that consumers will buy at prices that represent legitimate costs including "reasonable" profits, and that "legitimate" labor costs can be determined only by bargaining. This reasoning was clearly stated in some of the justification of N.R.A. practice. Though it was subscribed to by many business men, I believe that all experience reveals the consumer as the controlling factor, and that he will not, indeed cannot, pay prices, regardless of their "justification," if the value to him is less than the price. Costs have to be below value. The alternative is unemployment.

In considerable degree it seems to me that these fundamental differences of opinion prejudice the consideration of the practical questions of industrial relations. Nevertheless, these practical questions would remain if there were no such differences about economics and social policy.

What does the practice of collective bargaining involve?

For men: (1) The promotion and conservation of bargaining power. This means organization, expense, coercion of individuals and minorities. (2) The maintenance of bargaining position. This means the withholding of cooperation with employers that would extend beyond the strict limits of an agreement — an arm's length working relationship — exaggerated emphasis upon jurisdictional questions, and expensive losses of time in connection with them. (3) Great attention to the tactics of bargaining. This means expensive professionalism, emphasis upon artificialities, exaggeration of details, promotion of lack of confidence and distrust, and polemic attitudes.

For management: (1) Maintenance of bargaining position. This means taking an unprogressive attitude regarding projects that would benefit men if successful because of the difficulty of retraction if there is failure. (2) Maintenance of tactical position. This means giving no inch because it might call for a mile, keeping in reserve things that can be offered in bargains, if necessary or asked for. (3) Development and reinforcement of the idea that labor is only a commodity to be bought in the market or by contract as cheaply as possible. (4) A non-cooperative state of mind, involving the minimum interest in the welfare of employees, and the minimum interest in individuals. (5) A cold-blooded attitude toward employment, lay-offs, and the merits of individuals. (6) Secrecy, distrust, and unwillingness to recognize that employees have any stake or interest in the business.

What does the alternative "collective cooperation" involve?

For men: (1) Freedom from coercive conditions for individuals, groups or minorities, with absence of frictions and costs. (2) Lack of necessity for concentrating upon bargaining position, permitting attention to a cooperation concerning the real and basic interest of employees and the maintenance of a close and free working relationship, with freedom from jurisdictional questions and futile losses of time in connection with them; opportunity for attention to the real conditions of business and mutual adjustments to serve the interests of all. (3) Enhanced interest in work, confidence, stability.

For management: (1) Acceptance of responsibility for promoting practicable means of improving working conditions. (2) Concentration upon the progress of the business with a view to the advantages of all elements involved in it, as against all elements except labor. (3) Development of willingness to give the labor position more than an even break on new undertakings or in pioneering projects. (4) The development of a cooperative state of mind, maximizing the position of labor as more than merely a market or contract commodity, and permitting attention to the individual and groups, with recognition of the stake that employees have in a business or trade, and desire and willingness to avoid layoffs, etc.[2]

[2] An example of the importance of this attitude relates to individual job retraining in cases where employees are displaced or acquired skills are made obsolete by new technical developments. The easiest thing, perhaps sometimes the cheapest thing, for the employer is to drop such employees, recruiting as may be necessary from new labor sources. When artificial jurisdictional points of view are prominent it is very hard not to do this. When the employer is operating on the cooperative plan, he will retrain on his own initiative. It is the kind of thing which in any event cannot be successfully done by the employer except under a genuine cooperative relationship. It could not be "bargained" for in most cases because it requires a long plan of coordination with day by day technical operations. Yet the importance of this one subject to great numbers of employees probably exceeds all others relating to employment, either from the standpoint of stability of job or of earning capacity.

In short, the philosophy of collective bargaining is fundamentally opposed to cooperative attitudes and the development of sound personnel objectives, that of collective cooperation promotes the development of sound personnel practice and results. I am not making an artificial distinction without much real difference. The difference is great and important.

This difference of purpose and results is obscured by the current assumption that the argument all relates in the last analysis to the question of independent unions, which are of many varieties and conditions, as against "company" unions, which are likewise of many varieties and conditions. It is not my purpose generally and certainly not here to attempt to take a position in this debate. However, I do not hesitate to say that there now exist, and that there will continue to exist, independent unions in which the real spirit is one of collective cooperation, not collective bargaining. I do not decline to admit that there are "company" unions in which there does not exist a spirit of collective cooperation. It is certainly possible that "company" unions should be permeated with the bargaining idea. Generally, however, it must be admitted that independent unions can or will with difficulty maintain the cooperative idea; and it should be admitted that "company" unions will not easily maintain a bargaining attitude.

Moreover, I recognize that there are industries, particularly those most adapted to the "horizontal" type of union organization, in which employees must transfer frequently from one employer to another, where the conditions make collective cooperation difficult. I also understand perfectly well that there are industries or industrial managements in or with which it is not today possible really to work on a cooperative labor basis. These facts, if there were no others, would be sufficient grounds to justify legal permission to organize on a bargaining or combative basis, even though it accomplished no substantial or real advantage. That these facts justify compelling or attempting to compel collective bargaining when it is possible or where there already exists collective cooperation is emphatically denied. It seems like compelling barbarism where civilization already exists.

In this connection a word is warranted respecting an aspect of industrial relations that is hardly recognized by many. Those with experience with the management of organization know that in the daily work of industry the important group is what are called the intermediate and lower supervisory officials or employees — foremen, managers, department bosses, instructors, etc. Neither employers nor employees can function without the cooperation of this intermediate group. That they may do so the controllable conditions must be made such as recognize their capacities and limitations. The practice of collective bargaining usually, and I think necessarily, minimizes their function and responsibility in industrial relations, that of collective cooperation the reverse — it then can and does become a part of their job to promote the interest of employees. The idea that constructive work, leaving this group out of account, can be done by fiat is fantastic, whether the fiat be of Congress, legislature, employer, board of directors or executive.

To many, perhaps, my support of collective cooperation as the sound method of personnel relations will seem theoretical, visionary, idealistic. My answer is that in much of industry it has worked, and that for more than fifteen years I have seen it work in large organizations of which I was an executive. I have personal, practical experience with it. Far from perfect or even half developed, because both men and especially management require much time to become habituated to this method, I have nevertheless seen it accomplish for employees what no bargaining could accomplish or what bargainers would not even think of. What I say to you I have said to my own employees in nearly this language. They would, I think, say also the same in their own language.

*   *   *   *   *

In summation, I believe that progress in personnel relations involves recognition that the development of the individual employee is of first importance to which must be added chiefly the promotion of the will to collaborate. The essential first step in accomplishing these purposes is complete sincerity and honesty of employers and managers. The more general acceptance of these principles and a more general belief in their practicability depends upon the correction of false ideas concerning welfare work and concerning economic motives in business and the extent to which they do or can govern employee relations. In the choice of formal machinery of such relations, collective bargaining is weak or negative and permits only with difficulty the acceptance of these first principles, whereas collective cooperation is positive and conduces to, even forces, the use of these principles and the attainment of these purposes.

That, for the moment, organized efforts are being made to prevent real progress, under mistaken beliefs, must be admitted. That they may greatly retard the age of enlightenment in industrial relations is quite possible. That they can destroy what has already been accomplished I do not believe. Too many employers, too many employees, too many families, too much of society, already understands and subscribes to my own faith in these matters to permit inexperience, lack of knowledge, prejudice, or ulterior motives to destroy what they know to be good.[3]

[3] This last paragraph, as I reread this address after ten years, is the only one I would change, as respects substance. This now reads to me like wishful thinking. The Wagner Act really was the instrument for destroying what had been accomplished. It promoted industrial warfare, not industrial peace.

II

DILEMMAS OF LEADERSHIP IN THE
DEMOCRATIC PROCESS [1]

Two things are always to be observed; whether what is said is true in itself, or, being so, is applicable. In general, things are partly true, and partly not; in part applicable, and in part not. You are carefully therefore to distinguish; and to shew how far a thing is true and applies, and how far not. WILLIAM GERARD HAMILTON (*Parliamentary Logic,* about 1796)

THE subject I have been asked to discuss calls evidently for a critical and dispassionate examination of the limitations and faults of democratic institutions as they affect the selection, development, and conduct of leaders. Such an examination, however much needed, is nevertheless difficult because of the powerful sentiments and convictions that possess me. For I was born into the democratic faith and nurtured in the representative and republican institutions which arose from it. Those conditions which necessarily accompany democratic methods — such as high degrees of freedom of action and speech, some absolute civil rights of individuals, and certain kinds of social equality — are to me so fundamentally desirable that I would, if necessary, endure much bad government and make substantial material sacrifices to retain them for myself and family. Even were democracy in government to operate so badly as to be impracticable, I should regard the

[1] This paper was delivered as a Stafford Little Lecture at Princeton University in 1939. It was subsequently published by the University, under the University Extension Fund, Herbert L. Baker Foundation, with an introduction by Professor J. Douglas Brown, then Chairman, Public Lectures Committee, now Dean of the Faculty. It was distributed to all Princeton Alumni.

adoption of an alternative system as a choice of evils. Were I for any reason to be subject, perhaps with my own consent, to any other system in my own country, I should expect always to regret the extinction of a noble heritage from our fore-fathers, to suffer a great personal loss, and to experience the passing of a deep hope.

Notwithstanding this belief in democratic institutions, indeed even because of it, I undertake gladly the task assigned; for it seems to me that democracy in its broadest sense is not in danger of the power of other general systems of government, but of its own abuses, its blind worship of hopes and ideals unrelated to the facts of its own experience, its self-consuming lack of restraint in its greed for false application, its complacent love of the flattery of those who praise its faults and know not whereof they speak. The more gladly also because I believe the principle of democracy expresses an effort to superpose upon the unconscious and instinctive adaptations of men to men, so indispensable, an intelligence in cooperation secured from formal intellectual operations. The essential processes of democracy have now come to be applied more widely than ever. It would be a pity beyond all others if through abuse and disregard of right proportions we should fall back again upon the myth of the Great Hero and the fiction of the Absolute State in order that we might survive.

So far as possible, then, I shall avoid the common practice of discussing democracy or alternative systems in terms of political and social philosophies with large admixtures of phrases loaded with emotion and preconceptions of wide scope. I restrict my approach closely to attitudes in principle scientific rather than philosophical. I ask your attention to facts that are widely known, or available to public examination, and to inductions from common experience, susceptible to test by others than those who have drawn them.

Using this approach, I shall first define the essential process of democracy and suggest its significance and the criteria to be applied to it for purposes of this discussion; I shall then present some fundamental dilemmas of the democratic process, of two classes: first, those which are general and not especially related to leadership; and second, those directly affecting the number, quality, and behavior of leaders. Finally, I shall briefly discuss elementary bases of the selection of processes of governance, limitations of the use of the democratic process, the merits of that process under suitable conditions, and its dependence upon leaders of special qualities.

The Elements of Democratic Governance

Four propositions should first be presented as statements of fact.[2] One is that "democracy" relates to behavior *within* a cooperative system. There is certainly no question of democracy in an aggregate of hostile, opposed, isolated, or non-cooperative societies. The second fact is that democracy relates to governance and is some kind of system of making governing decisions. Third, democratic decisions are formal decisions, consciously arrived at by formal processes. They are not merely institutions resulting from informal interactions of individuals in a society. In other words, democracy is not merely societal, it is definitely governmental. The final proposition is that the efforts of a society formally and deliberately governed, as a whole, constitute a formal organization.[3] Democracy is or involves in general one of the available processes or sets of processes by which formal organizations may operate and maintain themselves.

There are many kinds of formal organizations. Political democracy refers to the governance of political organizations —

[2] They are in general developed in my book *The Functions of the Executive,* Harvard University Press, 1938, referred to hereinafter as *The Functions.*
[3] *The Functions,* chap. vi.

municipal corporations, states, and nations. Similarly, industrial democracy refers to industrial organizations, and religious democracy to religious organizations. Now we have had large experience with organizations. Each type has exemplified different systems of governance, so that there are ample bases for understanding the merits and limitations of these systems. This experience shows that a final test of any system of governance is the survival of the organization in which it is used. In other words, any such system to be good enough must at least "work." If an organization cannot survive, it is obvious that its system of governance perishes with it, and has no merit for that organization.

Survival depends upon two general factors: (1) the effectiveness of the system of governance as respects the *external* relations of the organizations; and (2) its *internal* efficiency, that is its capacity of securing cohesiveness, coordination, and subordination of concrete acts. Within wide limits these are mutually dependent factors./ A system that cannot determine what action will be effective does not enlist or maintain the requisite cohesiveness, coordination, and subordination, either because it fails or is believed to be failing./Conversely, a system that does not secure the necessary adherence and subordination and coordination of activities cannot direct action effectively. Thus the primary questions to be asked concerning every system of governance are: Does it adequately determine action adapted to the external conditions? Does it secure the subordination making such determinations effective?

THE ESSENTIAL DEMOCRATIC PROCESS

What is the system of governance known as democracy? In answering this question we are prone to include conditions believed prior necessities and also collateral or secondary consequences. For example, freedom of speech is regarded in most circumstances as necessary to democracy and also as one of its most cherished results. In this way the word "democracy" means many different things to different men. Indeed, attempted definitions of democracy which would comprehend what each of us feels about it would be too vague, as well as too lacking in general acceptance, for purposes of the present inquiry.

A common element, however, is observable in all "democracies." This is the use of a certain process in the making of at least some of the decisions affecting the whole of the cooperative body. This process is that of securing formal consent of an electorate to a formal governing proposition — a stated policy, a specific project, the election of a particular person to a specified position — the decision depending upon the numerical count of those consenting and of those dissenting. This is decision by vote. I have been unable even to conceive of any system of governance that would be called democratic without this kind of decision. With it there may or may not be something called "democracy," depending upon the personal attitudes of the observer, and such matters as the extent of the franchise, the scope or formal finality of the decisions, and the degree of freedom of the voters.

In organizations in which the franchise is not regarded by most of us as sufficiently wide to warrant using the term "democracy," it is nevertheless usually true that the democratic process is widely used. For example, the democratic process is employed in the election of a Pope; but the government of the Church is nevertheless absolute. Again, the directors of an industrial corporation are elected in legal principle by the stockholders, and the decisions of the boards of directors are likewise made by the democratic process; though few industrial corporations are regarded as democratic. Moreover, it may be true that even an absolute general government permits or requires subordinate organizations to be governed in some respects at least by a democratic process.[4] Contrariwise, in all large democracies there are vast numbers of formal decisions — especially administrative acts — which are not made by the democratic process.

Thus the use of a definition of a particular method of making decisions which have cooperative effect is more than a mere simplification of a confused conception; it greatly expands the field of observation and experience useful for investigation. For the essential democratic process has been widely used for a long time, and our experience with it is accordingly much greater than our experience with democracies. Indeed we might say that democracy depends upon the *degree* to which persons whose behavior is governed by common decisions formally participate by the democratic process in the making of such decisions.

THE FUNDAMENTAL TESTS OF THE DEMOCRATIC PROCESS

It will be well now to restate our primary questions. Does the democratic process adequately determine what ought to be done? Does it secure the subordination required effectively to execute governing decisions? Since these questions relate to factors that are mutually interacting, as already explained, it would be misleading to ask them separately, except with high precaution. They should rather be asked simultaneously; and when so asked we observe that democratic operations involve certain dilemmas.[5] Failure to make appropriate choices under these dilemmas in particular conditions or in certain types of

[4] For example, the charters of corporations by absolute governments may provide for general control by vote of stockholders or boards. Also, a considerable number of important decisions in armies may be made by boards and committees (though frequently with a final approval by the appointing authority).

[5] Systems of government are not the abstractions our discussions make of them, but are concrete events, and personal acts, largely habitual and emotional, involving conflicts. These conflicts, arising in the attempt to control events, are dilemmas. A dilemma is the necessity of choice emerging from

organizations or for specific purposes may be regarded as reflecting limitations either (1) of the democratic process or (2) of those who have the franchise or (3) of those who are leaders; or (4) inherent in the conditions themselves. However, since (1) method, (2) leaders, (3) voters, and (4) conditions are to a large extent mutually dependent and interacting factors, it would be incorrect or misleading in general to assign success or failure to any one of them. But a statement of the nature of some of the dilemmas may indicate approximately the character of the conditions of success or failure of the democratic process, and may point to the kind of efforts required to make it operate, or to the limits beyond which it has not yet been successfully operated.

Dilemmas Inherent in the Use of the Democratic Process

There are numerous dilemmas of the democratic method of superficial character which are commonly described as defects of democracy, such as criticisms that it involves irresponsibility; that it tends to irrelevant and trivial discussion and decisions; that it is ill-adapted to constructive initiative; that it is extravagantly expensive.

Such criticisms are unquestionably valid in some situations, but are not fairly to be made in some others. Defects probably arise from much more fundamental dilemmas present in the use of the democratic method under all conditions from small committees and boards in any kind of organization to the general elections of great democratic nations. Time permits discussion of four types: (1) the opposition between partial con-

---

action and situations of action. Indeed, they might often be called trilemmas, for the choice is not merely between newly recognized alternatives — the horns of a dilemma — but between making a choice and making none at all. In this sense, some choice, some resolution of the dilemma, is inevitable. In our consideration of these matters we need always to keep the feeling of the irresistible flow of vital action.

sent and complete conformance; (II) the discrepancy between abstract decision and concrete action; (III) time-lags; and (IV) political conflict.

I. THE DILEMMA OF CONSENT AND CONFORMANCE

The democratic method is one of decision by partial consent, whereas cooperative action requires substantially complete conformance. Thus the democratic process involves a fundamental conflict of principle. Although I believe this frequently evident in the behavior of leaders — political and others — it is seldom stated and is recognized by few. It is of great practical importance because it leads to false (ineffectual) decision, and thence to decreasing confidence in, or even abandonment of, the democratic process.

To persist or endure, any organization — whether a large nation, or a small organization of limited scope — must take action as a whole adapted to meet effectively the conditions of its environment; and the acts of the individuals must conform to these requirements. This conformance must be quite general and both positive and negative; that is, nearly every one must conform by doing the things required and by refraining from those forbidden. Thus the contrast between the process of coordinated effort and that of democratic decision is striking; for whereas cooperation means approximate unanimity of will, the democratic process means decision by division — by majorities and usually by small pluralities of those entitled to vote.

Such determinations can become effective in coordinated behavior only as, among other circumstances, faith in the democratic process leads to their acceptance as legitimately controlling the acts of individuals notwithstanding individual dissent. Such faith appears to have been generally insufficient except when (a) the franchise applied to persons of substantially similar status, similar beliefs, and similar emotional reactions; (*b*) certain fundamental personal rights were in practice excepted from the democratic process; and (*c*) personal interest in the maintenance of the organization counterbalanced other personal desires.

II. THE DILEMMA OF THE ABSTRACT AND THE CONCRETE

The second type of dilemma, closely related to the first, lies in the discrepancy between the abstract and the concrete, between the verbalization of ideas and the specific activities to which they refer.

The democratic is a process of decision in the form of a verbal statement. The issues are not only formally determined, but decisions are made by definite procedures of voting with specifications as to the franchise. Any decision so made is necessarily an abstract proposition. Even the choosing of a man for an office refers to a high abstraction unless the men nominated are well known to the voter and the nature of the job to be filled is very clearly understood — not merely by knowledge of a formal prescription of duties, but by an experiential understanding of the character of the daily work required and the conditions under which it is done. Obviously democratic decisions are likely to be least abstract in small organizations and extremely abstract in large organizations, as, for example, in large nations.

Thus the democratic process is one for determining consent or dissent to intellectual abstractions. But conformance, upon which the effectiveness of organization depends, relates to concrete acts of individuals. The distinction between the conformance of the acts of individuals and the acceptance by individuals of abstract propositions, though well known, is often neglected despite its importance. Even with unanimous consent there may be marked failure of action to conform to decision. The Eighteenth Amendment was adopted by nearly all the States by votes of their legislatures and probably expressed general popular assent to this proposition. Yet many who assented did not conform. Again, those who elect men to positions of leadership often do not follow their "leaders."

The inconsistency between decision by majority or plurality consent to abstract propositions and approximately complete conformance of concrete behavior is inherent. All general decision is abstract and relates to the future. It necessarily involves an estimate of undisclosed details. Further, the enormous complex of action which is covered by a general decision is in detail beyond the comprehension and the imagination of men.[6] Hence, this dilemma may be stated as the conflict between conscious socio-intellectual propositions and the unconscious physiological or biological propensities of individuals conditioned by present organization action and by past social experience. Thus men often agree to do what in fact is beyond their physical, mental, or emotional capacities. They accept in the abstract as desirable that which they find in reality to be undesirable or even painful. They often refuse or avoid action that is repugnant to them without knowing why, though they have formally consented to it.

Since the type of dilemma under consideration is present in all formal (verbalized) decision, it may be asked in what respects it differs under the democratic as against an autocratic process. The differences lie (1) in the superior *position* of judgment of individual leaders, officials, or executives in relation to concrete conditions; and (2) in the relatively irrevocable character of democratic decisions.

1. Decisions of responsible individuals are made largely on the basis of a *sense of the situation,* involving elements of unconscious and non-intellectual reactions and habits below the level of abstractions. Experienced leaders, like experienced physicians, are frequently able to "diagnose" conditions cor-

[6] From this fact arises much of the business of our courts.

rectly, though unable quickly or even at all to formulate intelligible reasons for their judgments. In contrast, the unconscious and non-intellectual reactions of individual voters are not and usually cannot be well integrated with the situations to which the propositions apply upon which they are voting. Their reactions are usually integrated with quite different situations. This is partly a matter of position and partly of degree of personal responsibility. "Everybody" cannot be in the most advantageous position to judge; and "what is everybody's business is nobody's business."

2. However, the importance of this type of dilemma lies only partly in mere conflict between a predominant abstract opinion and the requirements of concrete action. Indeed, such conflict obtains even in individual thought and action also. The crucial dilemmas arise from the fact that a democratic decision as a concrete event conflicting with others is difficult to reverse promptly. A common method of avoiding such conflicts is, therefore, to disregard the decision. Hence, there is a persistent tendency of the democratic process to create illegality and thus to destroy itself.

III. THE DILEMMA OF TIME-LAG

A third type of dilemma relates to the time-lags involved between the need for action and decision; and between decision and corresponding execution. This needs only brief discussion here. There are three stages: (1) delay in recognizing the need for decision; (2) time required in making it; and (3) time necessary for promulgating and inculcating it.

1. Obviously a need for many important decisions often arises suddenly out of the stream of events and action. The democratic process is at best slow. Every organization that depends upon the action of committees and boards is aware of this. Quite effective — but usually illegal — techniques are often necessary to get prompt answers by circumventing the

democratic process. Solutions so obtained are ordinarily accepted without question except in some cases when the result is disliked or the person who is responsible is disliked. The responsibility involved, however, frequently leads to failure to decide by any method whatever with sufficient promptness — a fact often difficult to observe.

2. Committee chairmen or legislative leaders — and many others — know how long the democratic process of decision almost always is. But the element of indecisiveness thereby involved is one of the most destructive of influences in cooperation, a fact that appears to be not well understood. Not only is the effective timing of action often impossible, but delay depresses the initiative and enthusiasm required for the proper execution of decisions.

3. The importance of delay in promulgating decisions will not be appreciated by those who do not know that cooperative behavior is largely instructed, practised, habitual, and timed behavior.

In cases where the time-lag of the democratic process is generally recognized as important, as in emergencies (it is often important but not generally so recognized), the common solution is to abandon the democratic process under some disguise or legal fiction.

To be sure, time-lag of serious proportions is very often observed where autocratic processes are used. The reasons for this fact are sufficiently comprehended for present purposes in the statement that they are due to the personal incapacity of an individual under the conditions for the making of decisions. The difficulty lies in the competence of individuals and in the effectiveness with which the systems of governance and the emotions of followers permit the development and selection of those competent to decide. It does not lie directly in the autocratic process itself. On the other hand, no matter how competent may be the members of an electorate for the opera-

tion of the democratic process or the leaders of a group operating democratically, time-lag *is inherent in the democratic
process itself.* This is the important point to note and seems
to me to be the clearest of all facts regarding alternative systems of decision having cooperative effect.

The point is well demonstrated by Locke in his chapter "Of
Prerogative" in his *Treatise on Civil Government.* What he
says in effect is that in many circumstances it is impossible effectively to apply the democratic process and that decisions
must be made by the executive either because of the absence
of a decision made democratically or notwithstanding a decision so made. His chapter is largely a rationalization of facts,
which he cannot escape, so that these facts may fit into his
general theory of civil government. He is merely stating that
in addition to the numerous secondary decisions of detail,
which are tacitly accepted as necessarily performed by autocratic processes, it is necessary that some major decisions in a
generally democratic system also be made autocratically. He
does not use the phrase "time-lag" and this is, of course, not
the only factor involved; but it is evident that time-lag is what
he largely has in mind, for he says in the first paragraph that
the executor of laws has the right "by the common law of nature" to use a certain power *"till* the legislative can *conveniently* be assembled to provide for it." (My emphasis.)
Again, he says "for since many accidents may happen," etc.
The same idea of time-lag is also implicit in paragraph 167 [7]
in explaining the prerogative of the King to summon Parliament where he says "for it being impossible to foresee which
should always be the fittest place for them to assemble in, and
what the best season, the choice of these was left with the executive power," etc.

[7] D. Appleton-Century Company, 1937 edition.

IV. THE DILEMMA OF POLITICAL CONFLICT

The fourth general dilemma of the democratic process and the last to be presented here is that it *disorganizes* by inciting political conflict.

The democratic process involves discussion. The meaning of a proposition has to be stated. The form of statement is that of reasons, and the conditions of statement are usually those of debate. Indeed, the opportunity for fair and full discussion has often been asserted to constitute an important merit of the democratic process.

The point to be noted here is not that men disagree as to what should or should not be done but as to *reasons*. Thus they will often follow decisions "made by authority" without reasons, as "reasonable" and practicable, or more often without a thought, since they take no responsibility; but will be unable to "agree" (except by narrow majorities or pluralities) if they themselves have to participate in the decision. Nor is this merely captious or arbitrary. A formulated general decision is a symbol not only of projected concrete action. It also inevitably symbolizes a philosophy of action to each of those participating in the decision. It may be true that differences of philosophy are even more important sources of discord than differences of material interest.

This scarcely needs to be labored. To give only one type of example, it is manifested by the elaborate techniques of political tactics — the imputing of false motives to men, the drawing of certain kinds of "red herrings." While the effect most to be emphasized here is the disruption of organization, other important alternative effects are on decision itself. To avoid political conflict often requires weak compromises or results in failure to make some decisions urgently needed. Evidence of these facts is not only continuously presented in our public affairs, but also in operations of private boards, committees, and assemblies.[8]

*   *   *   *   *

This statement of fundamental dilemmas of the democratic process might lead some persons unjustifiably to regard it as a damning indictment of that process. But all other methods of governance are likewise replete with dilemmas, though I cannot discuss them here. Some, like the opposition between partial consent and complete conformance and the discrepancy between abstract decision and concrete action, are in principle common to all systems. Here what we need to remember is that the democratic process is not exempt from such dilemmas — a fact that blind partisans of democracy are prone to neglect. Other dilemmas equally important are peculiar to each system. Thus a complete statement of these dilemmas would enable us to see that the choice of systems is the underlying problem. The relative significance of the dilemmas inherent in each process is to be appraised in conjunction with the conditions of its application; and also in conjunction with the availability

[8] The evidence is perhaps not conveniently available as respects private affairs, except to those who have considerable personal experience. It is my opinion that in those cases where there is dereliction of duty by boards of directors it may often be due to unwillingness of responsible men to inject the political effects of divisions of formal votes on the organization involved. Granted that this reluctance sometimes has pernicious results, the fact remains that on the whole the reticence as regards introducing political conflict by divided votes is in most cases justified. The specific "errors" resulting (and they may be compensating errors) are not so serious as would be the political effects of division. Most of those who are critical of the records of industrial boards of directors are naturally unaware of this and fix their attention on the "pathological" cases with no knowledge of the "physiology" involved. Although the range of disturbing conditions is much wider in public than in commercial organizations, the criteria of success or failure are much more exacting in the latter, and the margins usually much narrower. Hence, a degree of political disturbance which is perhaps tolerable in many public organizations may be fatal in most commercial organizations.

of suitable organization leaders. For it is the final function of leaders to solve organization dilemmas.

THE DILEMMAS OF LEADERS

Leaders as functioning elements of organization are not formally nominated, selected, elected, or appointed, nor are they born to leadership; they are accepted and followed; and are sometimes pressed or (rarely) coerced into leading. Indeed, I have never observed any leader who was able to state adequately or intelligibly why he was able to be a leader, nor any statement of followers that acceptably expressed why they followed. Also leaders historically and logically precede all systems of formal organization decision. They have been primary factors in the selection or adoption of every system of governance; but once established, such a system becomes a conditioning element of the functions of leaders and also a means by which their functions are carried out. This arises from the facts that positions of control are essential to the coordination of effort — a common element in all systems of governance; and that leaders must operate chiefly through such formal positions.[9] Thus the dilemmas which confront leaders are of two classes: (1) those of the general types, already presented, which leaders have to solve; and (2) those that directly affect the selection and behavior of leaders and the reactions of their followers to them. Three types of these will now be discussed, as follows: (I) Appropriate aim with effective action and politics; (II) Leadership and executive position, and (III) Diffusion of responsibility.

I. THE DILEMMA OF EFFECTIVE ACTION AND POLITICS

In an autocratic system of governance every leader or executive is constantly confronted with the dilemma involved in the

---

[9] *The Functions,* chap. xv, pp. 217–23.

fact that a specific aim most appropriate to the *purpose* of organization effort is in some degree out of accord with the means available for its accomplishment, that is, the human beings whose efforts are to be utilized. The choice to be made usually requires some modification of the ideal aim to one adapted to the capacities, emotions, and wills of the individuals whose efforts must accomplish it; and simultaneously some modification of the latter by training, precept, example, and inspiration. Thus there are involved initially nice questions of judgment of a technical character as to the range of acceptable aims on one side, and on the other, concerning the capacities and dispositions of the persons whose efforts are involved. Taking into account these preliminary judgments, leaders reach decisions in detail as to precise aims and as to the definite instructions, persuasion, and inducements necessary for effective cooperative effort. These decisions call for intimate knowledge and intuitive understanding based on experience, concentration, and skill on the part of the leader both as respects the technical situation and the human resources, that is, the individuals and groups whose efforts are to be utilized.

Either of the horns of such dilemmas usually will be modified where the democratic process is employed. The aim may be determined by this process, or the means — for example, the number of persons and rates of pay. The initial dilemma of the leader should be usually conceived as not relieved by democratic decision in either respect.[10] The task still remains of coordinating numerous efforts with precision to obtain a concrete effect. Indeed, it can readily be observed that the dilemma is frequently made more severe. Decision as to one part of the problem is often made without attention to the other part, because the requisite intimate knowledge and concentration

[10] Usually, in general, not always. As later noted, sometimes the process of formal assent is an important and even necessary aid in securing willing subordination.

and sense of the situation are not available to the individual participants in the democratic process. That process therefore in general adds a second dilemma to the initial one. It creates for the leader a trilemma. He must seek a concrete program of action which is at once adapted (*a*) to the technical (external) situation; (*b*) to the internal operative organization condition; and (*c*) to at least the majority abstract "democratic" opinion, and usually also to the minority opinions, both as to aim and means. The latter is the political factor. In principle it is ineradicable from the democratic process.[11]

The complication introduced by the political factor is so great that it has heretofore made impossible the direct use of the democratic method in determining most concrete activities. The exclusion of a wide field of activities from the application of the democratic process is so much a matter of course and so little consciously perceived that this statement of the nature of the political complications may seem theoretical and remote from observable events. However, it is well known that committees, boards, and legislatures frequently determine upon aims which cannot be accomplished under the conditions, or prescribe means which prevent their accomplishment, or establish conditions which destroy the power of effective leadership.

It is probable that unfavorable consequences of the political factor can rarely be avoided and that many situations theoretically available to the democratic process are for this sole reason not practicable of solution by it. The reasons are clear. The addition of the political to the more primitive factors of cooperative effort adds greatly to the complexities of leadership. These complexities may be regarded for illustration as increasing as the cube of the number of factors involved, so that they might be stated as of the order of three times as great under the democratic process as under an autocratic method. After

[11] It is in some degree usually present in any other process.

much observation, due consideration, and some personal experience, I am of the opinion that the comparative difficulties of leadership under the democratic process are, in fact, of this order, having in mind the same standard of accomplishment of specific aims or of general aims where only short periods of time, say five years, are involved. Stated in reverse form, I believe the more general the purpose and the longer the period of time, the less important are the complications of leadership under the democratic process, *provided leaders in quantity and quality can be obtained to survive the short period burdens.*

This means that the democratic process in general will be less effective and less efficient, at least for short time periods, than autocratic processes *unless the quantity of leaders is greater and their quality better than would be otherwise sufficient.* It would be a great disservice to the ideal of democracy to underestimate this.

II. THE DILEMMA OF PERSONALITY AND POSITION

Effective leadership in organizations depends upon *leaders* of appropriate qualities on one hand and *a system of positions* to be filled by them on the other — upon communicators in communication positions.[12] Usually only a few alternative schemes of communication or of official organization may be regarded as practicable at a given time; and usually personnel available is limited. The most suitable combination of positions and personnel requires modification of the scheme of positions on one hand to meet the limitations of personnel, and on the other hand the selection of personnel with respect to the available schemes of communication. This is a fundamental problem of all cooperative effort under *any* method of governance. In the democratic process the dilemmas arise chiefly from three sources: (1) the scheme of positions must be rela-

---

[12] *The Functions,* chap. xii, pp. 172–81.

tively rigid; (2) the selection of leaders must be based in part upon political as distinguished from organizing abilities; (3) the subtleties in the precise combining of leader and official position are generally beyond the capacities of any democratic system.

1. Regarding the scheme of positions, it is clear that under any plan of operations it must usually be stable, not only from the standpoint of the convenience of administration but also from the standpoint of the habituation of organization and especially of the stability of constituent unit organizations.[18] But under the democratic process the changing of the scheme of positions introduces not merely confusion of ideas but also the political elements. Is it not apparent that this results in archaic administrative systems in democracies, and that reorganization is rarely effected without upheavals of serious proportion or difficult and disorganizing political conflicts?

2. Since leaders under the democratic process must function with respect to the political factor in addition to others, it is obvious that political abilities become important qualifications. But the appraisal of the latter by the democratic process is necessarily confused by lack of unity and the division into groups and parties which it probably requires. The difficulties are apparent. It is a generally valid criticism of the democratic process that it is relatively ineffective in selecting men on their merits for organization positions. (Perhaps political party organization positions should be excluded from this statement.)

3. This difficulty need not be ascribed solely to the party element in the democratic process. The extreme delicacy of the judgment of abilities required in complex situations and the destructive effect of open discussion of such matters on confidence itself — both of leaders and followers — are even more important, in my opinion, than the more obvious and tangible difficulties.

[18] *Ibid.*, chap. viii, p. 104.

The democratic process involves not only a diffusion of responsibility within an electorate, but in addition it requires that leaders shall carry out policies of others. They are publicly blamed for faults not their own; and conversely, they are credited with false merits. Their influence with their followers is thereby weakened. Thus this process restricts the initiative, enthusiasm, and confidence of leaders and followers and greatly reduces the incentives to leaders and their personal responsibility. The quality of leadership is reduced, and the quantity of leaders narrowed, under the very conditions which require that both should be increased.

There is a general disposition of the public and also of many politicians and public officials to assume insufficiency of leadership capacity upon the part of public officials appointed by the democratic process or of those directly dependent upon those so appointed. In my opinion the deficiency is at least greatly exaggerated. I do not rely upon such sentiments here. A small *proportion* of leadership positions is today filled by the democratic process — chiefly major public officials, officers of labor organizations, social organizations; also principal officers of corporations and universities — but as to these classes the process is often nominal. This makes it quite possible that adequate leadership is available in this limited degree despite the depressive effect of the democratic process on the ambitions of persons otherwise competent to lead. The important measure of the effect of the irresponsibility of the democratic process would only be indicated by what we might expect if a large proportion of important organization positions were to be filled by this process. I believe that a much wider extension of the democratic process to the formally organized efforts of our society — so far as appointments are concerned — would quickly break down through the inability to secure the much higher quality and quantity of leaders then necessary. It should be noted that the proportion of positions filled democratically has probably been decreasing in major degree in recent years due to the extension of civil service systems, the development of large-scale corporations, the exceedingly "practical" methods of continuity of tenure in some other organizations, the increasing extent of perfunctory legislative approvals of "career" men, and the rapid spread of "administrative law," not only in government but — under other conceptions or names — in corporations.

It may not be clear why the *quantity* of leaders is so much affected. This arises partly from the greatly increased time required of leaders by the democratic process — their exposure to trivial or embarrassing interviews or interpellations, for example. It also arises from the necessities of purely political organization and the mechanical aspects of the democratic process — the voting process, meetings fixed in advance, etc.

* * * * *

It would be shamefully stupid to underrate the dilemmas of the democratic process as they affect the selection and development of leaders or as they discourage followers, thereby diminishing cohesion and coordination. They are by no means decisive when contrasted with the corresponding dilemmas of other processes, and for many situations the democratic process seems clearly superior to others. But probably for many situations it is so inferior that it is in practice impossible, and this should be definitely recognized.

THE ADOPTION OF SYSTEMS OF GOVERNANCE

Notwithstanding that in practice the democratic process is persistently subject to major dilemmas such as I have described, yet this process is widely used with success and satisfaction. However, a similar statement may be made respecting other methods of government. What determines fundamentally the choices in great and small organizations? How is it that the democratic process is adopted when no democracy is available to determine its adoption? How is it that it is abandoned despite the interests that become vested in it? In what way are determined the limits of fictions and of circumventions attendant upon the democratic process — and upon others as well — that seem to permit their nominal retention notwithstanding their *de facto* abandonment?

The answer to these questions refers to the informal processes of cooperation that underlie all formal processes. The answer is that the formal system is confirmed by the conformatory behavior of leaders and followers jointly. A silent "democracy of behavior" determines all systems of government, public or private. Not what the King says but how he acts, not what his subjects say but what they do, determines this question. If he in fact leads, and they in fact follow, he is King, they are subjects. And if they call him King and themselves subjects, but decide their course by a Parliament and execute it through its leaders, they are using the democratic method. What men will and can do decides the issue. They can and will use the democratic process under some conditions; they cannot or will refuse to do so under others. In conditions of complexity, or great danger, or rapidity of action, they have rarely been willing or able to follow a committee or to elect a leader, as for example in battle. John Locke [14] clearly recognized this when he said that there can be no judge on earth to determine for the specific condition whether prerogative, i.e., the autocratic process, is properly used as against the democratic process, although the people by informal processes "have reserved that ultimate determination to themselves which belongs to all mankind, where there lies no appeal on earth, by a law antecedent and paramount to all positive laws of men . . ."

[14] *Treatise on Civil Government*, "Of Prerogative," final paragraph.

If a system once accepted destroys that mutual adaptation of behavior of leaders and followers — either because it reaches ineffective decisions, or destroys leadership or divides followers — then disorganization, schism, rebellion, or conformance to a new system ensues. This is a doctrine, however, that no formal government whether autocratic or democratic, public or private, can apparently admit in principle, without destruction of the sense of legality and legitimacy which cooperating men seem universally to require. This is the fundamental dilemma of all systems of governance.[15]

LIMITATIONS OF DEMOCRACY

Hitherto men seem to have studied democracy chiefly from the standpoint of the ideals of individual development, of freedom of individuals from the tyranny of disorganization of autocratic systems that were decadent, that no longer commanded loyalty, that produced ineffective leadership. But as I have said in the beginning, democracy is dependent upon the method of *cooperative* formal decision. This is clearly a process of organizations, not of individuals, and needs to be studied first from this point of view; for history shows that democracy too can destroy the freedom of individuals by a tyranny of indecision, of disorganization, no longer commanding loyalty, decadent, lacking leadership of the highest order which it requires. Can it never happen to us as it has in other lands, and as the ancients said it always would in its turn? We do not know because we watch the stars and forget the ground we walk upon.

Yet even now it seems to me we can state a few broad limits of the democratic process and at the same time a few broad merits — with which suggestions I close.

The democratic process, whether for nations or small organizations, appears to be ineffective and incapable of com-

[15] Cf. *The Functions*, chap. xii, "The Theory of Authority."

manding loyalty when the franchise is extended to individuals of widely diverse races, religions, capacities or interests, *unless* matters of race, creed, and economic interest of *individuals* are within broad limits excluded from direct and from important indirect decisions made by the democratic method. This exclusion must be by constitution or by social habits not alterable without nearly unanimous consent and conformance both. Thus either religious freedom or religious uniformity, either actual absence of racial discrimination or complete exclusion of some races, and individual economic freedom or substantial economic equality are necessary conditions of the democratic franchise.

Again matters of urgent speed, of highly technical character, of profound intellectual content, or of very complex conscious coordination, must in practice be excluded from the democratic process except in most general terms.

Moreover, a considerable capacity for abstract thought, that is, for reading, writing, and speaking is necessary. Excepting for small organizations, where decison is very closely related to concrete conditions, the democratic method is not suitable for the illiterate; but marked diversity of education and of intellectual intelligence is also not conducive to the use of this method. Wide expansion of the degrees of education, the minute specialization of knowledge and of function are unfavorable conditions.

Again, there must be such restrictions of the fields of decision or of their details that the number of decisions to be taken democratically is not large. The tediousness and slowness of the process are notorious, the difficulty of maintaining interest nearly obvious, its costliness apparent. I think it likely to be generally conceived at some later time that there is an optimum proportion of decisions in a given organization that can be made by democratic methods, or conversely by other methods. This would differ depending upon the purpose and character of the organization, and the conditions which would also be variable. Such a conception would lead to more discriminating judgment as to the field of application or as to the character of questions to which the democratic process may best apply.

MERITS OF THE DEMOCRATIC PROCESS

Where the conditions and the desires permit the operation of the democratic process, and it is restricted to those conditions, it has, I believe, great advantages, especially in the field of general government. These are that it offers in the long run greater probability of adequate higher leadership, if confined to major positions, than either the principle of heredity or of power; and permits succession to the highest positions with decreased probability of disruption. Again, it is a process that may be used to inspire solidarity of organization by avowed consent, and to increase the sense of participation, which are especially important when habits and preconceptions of people must change. The plebiscites of dictators are of significance in this connection. And, finally, the relative freedom of action, thought and speech necessary to the democratic process develops a wider sense of personal responsibility, and initiative and adaptability in individuals. This permits greater flexibility of organization and capacity for adaptation that are important for the meeting of great organization crises. When, also, people value these things so much that they will attend to the duties of participation in the democratic process, it is a way of living with others that is loved for its own sake and provides a satisfaction of high order. Democracy then becomes in that aspect not a means but an end in itself. Only so can men have necessary faith in an abstract system which in the long last must be greater than the loyalty they grant to leaders. However, history shows the folly of supposing that an ineffective system of government — democratic or autocratic — can survive as an exclusive end in itself.

The Qualities of Democratic Leadership

Although faith in the democratic system is essential to its use, and must be superior to the wavering loyalties of men to men, yet without leaders neither democracy nor any system of governance can survive. In any system those who lead must possess in some combination acceptable to their followers the capacities of discerning what ought to be done and of how it can be done by those who follow them. But in democracies a veritable aristocracy of leadership is required. As Bryce, the friend of democracy, once said: "Thus Free Government cannot but be, and has in reality always been, an Oligarchy within a Democracy." [16] The democratic process either in government or in innumerable other organizations in which it may be used, depends upon leaders strong enough to maintain their ambition under its perplexities, patient to endure its restraints, proud to be foremost among the free, humbly loyal to the humble, wise enough to seek service above the illusions of power and the futilities of fame, willing to be briefly spent in the long span of marching events. Among you, I have believed, there are many, warned of the dilemmas of the democratic process, who will see the greater challenge and the wider meaning of the service of leadership which democracy has given to us in America.

[16] *Modern Democracies*, The Macmillan Company, 1921, Vol. II, p. 550.

III

RIOT OF THE UNEMPLOYED AT
TRENTON, N. J., 1935[1]

INTRODUCTION

IN 1935 when I was serving for the second time as State Director of the New Jersey Relief Administration, I had an experience of negotiating with the leaders of the organized unemployed recipients of relief in Trenton, N. J., before, during, and subsequent to a serious "relief" riot. I presented and analyzed this experience as a case in concrete sociology in lectures at Harvard College in 1938, 1939, 1940, and twice in 1941 in an experimental course known as "Sociology 23." I gave the same lecture in 1941 at the Harvard Medical School in a similar course intended to orient the medical student to the social background of the practice of medicine; and in 1938 I also presented the same material, but in the language of the "shop," at a meeting in New York of the chief executives of the Bell Telephone System.

I believe this case will be of interest to many of my friends — both university men and men of affairs. I have not made it available in printed form sooner because it involves some criticism of the Relief Administration and because I was reluctant to run any risk of appearing to make the representatives of the unemployed "guinea pigs" in a public way. The lapse of ten years now makes it unlikely that any embarrassment will

---

[1] Although this paper was first prepared in 1938, it was not even privately distributed until much later. Circumstances in 1945 seemed to call for making it available in printed pamphlet form. It is reproduced here with the Introduction written September 10, 1945.

follow its restricted publication. The case was not reduced to writing until after my first lecture in 1938. I emended it slightly after experience in subsequent lectures chiefly by adding footnotes; and I have now added some longer notes for reasons which will be apparent shortly. In addition, it is desirable to give briefly the setting of the lecture, its purpose, and some conditions determining its style and form.

In 1937 the late Professor Lawrence J. Henderson undertook to develop an experimental course in "Concrete Sociology." Its immediate aim was to present to students a number of concrete cases of human interaction and behavior in social situations, to convey to them something of the nature of such situations, and to furnish thereby illustrations of scientific approach to problems of human relations. To this end Professor Henderson enlisted the aid of about thirty men, — faculty members and lawyers, physicians and men of affairs, each of whom agreed to present one or more cases. In so far as possible it was desired that each individual presenting a case should personally have been a participant in it or an immediate observer of it, or, if the case was historically remote, should have a complete familiarity with its known facts. The reason for this specification was Dr. Henderson's belief that progress in the social sciences required intimate familiarity with the concrete material of the subject, an experience lacking heretofore in the great majority of social scientists. His views were well expressed in the following excerpts from the last draft of his first lecture in the course, sent to me in August 1941.

After quoting Aristotle, Sainte-Beuve, Chesterfield, Sainte Aulaire, Gouverneur Morris, and Hazlitt, to the effect that understanding in the social field is not possible without experience, he went on:

Some years ago a young Oxford don came to the conclusion that men who have missed the highest academic prizes and gone out into the world seem, thirty years after when they come back to Oxford, better men than their successful competitors who have stayed on to lead the academic life. He was so much struck by this contrast that he resigned his fellowship and left Oxford. An English scholar who has become an administrator of public affairs, and therefore knows both the academic life and the life of affairs, told this tale. In reply, it was suggested that it is not merely experience of the world which changes and develops men in this way, but still more the practice of deciding and acting under the burden of responsibility for the consequences. This suggestion was unhesitatingly accepted. Indeed, observation and experience clearly indicate that nothing contributes more to the difference that Aristotle recognized between men of action and theorists than practice or lack of practice in deciding and acting under the burden of responsibility.

The man who has the habit of action under responsibility is deeply modified and differently oriented because of this experience. It is not too much to say that his whole organism is in a different state from that of a person who has not the habit of action under responsibility. This is not conceived, and can only with difficulty be imagined, by young, inexperienced students, or even in many cases by theorists who without practical experience have devoted much study to a subject. But unless a man, young or old, is aware of the importance of this psycho-physiological adaptation, that is, of the nature and effect of certain kinds of conditioned reflexes and of the way in which both action and understanding are thereby modified, he can hardly understand many aspects of the interactions between men.

Accordingly, Aristotle's criticism may still be made, more than two thousand years after, of much of our current political science *and, in general, medicine only excepted, of the branches of science that are conversant with experiences and affairs of daily life,* that is to say, with events in which interactions between persons are important. Meanwhile, medicine has progressed. Why?

Aristotle's explanation may still be given. In the complex business of living as in medicine *both* theory and practice are necessary conditions of understanding, and the method of Hippocrates is the only method that has ever succeeded widely and generally. The first element of that method is hard, persistent, intelligent, responsible, unremitting labor in the sick room, not in the library: the all-round adaptation of the doctor to his task, an adaptation that is far from being merely intellectual. The second element of that method is accurate observation of things and events, selection, guided by judgment born of familiarity and experience, of the salient and the recurrent phenomena, and their classification and methodical exploitation. The third element of that method is the judicious construction of a theory — not a philosophical theory, nor a grand effort of the imagination, nor a quasi-religious dogma, but a modest pedestrian affair, or perhaps I had better say, a useful walking-stick to help on the way — and the use thereof. All this may be summed up in a word: The physician must have, first, intimate, habitual, intuitive familiarity with things; secondly, systematic knowledge of things; and thirdly, an effective way of thinking about things. His intuitive familiarity must embrace his systematic knowledge and his way of thinking as well as the things he studies. Without these three qualifications no man can be trusted to think scientifically. It is one of the broadest of inductions that competent men of science are no more logico-experimental than other men when they step outside the field in which they have acquired intuitive familiarity with things.

In a footnote to the last paragraph above, Dr. Henderson quoted Galileo (from his "Dialogues Concerning Two New Sciences") as follows:

Indeed, I myself, being curious by nature, frequently visit [the arsenal of Venice] . . . for the mere pleasure of observing the work of those who, on account of their superiority over other artisans, we call "first rank men." Conference with them has often helped me in the investigation of certain effects including not only those which are striking, but also those which are recondite and almost incredible.

As these passages suggest, Dr. Henderson, whose career had been chiefly that of a physiologist and teacher at the Harvard Medical School, believed that the methods of study and teaching in social science should be similar to those which experience had shown to be good in medical research and training. Since laboratories and controlled experiment are of little application in the social sciences, except psychology, this means that the approach should correspond to that of clinical investigation and teaching of medicine and surgery. Thus the cases presented in Sociology 23 were somewhat like clinical material.[2]

[2] This should not be understood as suggesting that Dr. Henderson supposed that the technique of physician-patient or counselor-client relationships is ap-

Accordingly, though it had to be post facto demonstration, my case, as I presume others, was presented somewhat as at a clinic in which I was operating, explaining to students what I diagnosed, what I was doing, what reactions I observed, what I thought about it in terms of a conceptual scheme known to the students. One of the objects of my case was to show how difficult but important this clinical method is in social science.

The conceptual scheme, "the effective way of thinking about things," taught in the introductory lectures was largely based on Pareto's sociology as presented in the English translation under the title *The Mind and Society.* I had for several years been a student of Pareto's work. I also had collaborated very extensively with Dr. Henderson in developing the introductory lectures, so that I was thoroughly familiar with them. The manner of presentation of my case was determined thereby. It is not necessary, however, to have any knowledge of Pareto or to have read the introductory lectures to read this case, as the notes I have added will supply, I believe, all that is needed.

RIOT OF THE UNEMPLOYED AT TRENTON, N. J., 1935

A CASE IN CONCRETE SOCIOLOGY

The case I present to you this afternoon is one of which I have direct intimate personal knowledge. In fact, as will be evident, what I know of it comes from the fact that I was myself a leading participant in the events to be described. This deserves emphasis at the outset, because its significance in this case is typical of many others of importance for sociology. By this I mean that a mere description of the events as seen by a keen observer having no knowledge of the forces at play would

---

plicable generally in the study of human relations. The emphasis here is not on a special method but upon acquiring familiarity with material by working in or with it.

be a bare recital of acts, incomplete, probably misleading, and possibly quite erroneous, because of the omission of the understanding and the intentions of the participants, although it might be dramatic and the acts even attended by important consequences. A part of the point of this observation lies in the fact that in many instances, including the case at hand, the mere introduction of such an observer into the situation would itself be a sufficient change of circumstances to radically alter the cases. It will be evident to you, I think, that had a person been present not himself a "real party" in the events, the behavior of none could have been the same as it was and probably would have been greatly different as to some of the participants. Every one would have "played up" to such an observer in some degree, and all would have been conscious that a "record" was being made. Hence, in many situations in which social forces are at work direct objective observation is either necessarily deficient or even destructive of the data.

The alternative, as in the case I give you, presents the other horn of the dilemma. The statements of participants certainly are capable of describing many of the overt acts involved, and in addition much of the understanding of the participants, and of their intentions, especially those of the relator. But such statements are subjective. They are often interpretive of events much more than descriptive of events. They are notoriously unreliable, and can only be safely used, like the patient's statement of symptoms, by one skilled in interpreting such statements and possessed of a thorough knowledge and experience. This is especially true in cases like the present because, for the reasons already stated, unless interpretation of intentions, i.e., of the subjective elements involved, is given, the substance of the case is largely omitted. The directly observable action of many social situations can only be made significant for sociological and other purposes by statement in terms of emotions, interests, intentions, of which the action is the manifestation.

This leads to the final difficulty of most importance. What I have said so far is understood and in principle accepted by most of us. What I now say is not understood and accepted by many. It is that necessarily the description, in its analytical portions at least, is pure rationalization. I shall tell you that I diagnosed the situation in this or that way, that I intended this or that, that I reacted in this or that way, that I produced this or that effect, that others were affected in this or that way, etc. This is all concocted by me after the events. When the action was taking place I had almost no time for rational processes. Both my action and that of others was necessarily responsive, intuitive, emotional. I believe this is always, or nearly always, so in social situations in which the necessity of numerous and almost instantaneous decisions is imposed on the participants within a short period of time.

I should warn you that this does not necessarily mean that either knowledge intellectually acquired, or intellectual or logical thinking processes had no part in the action. On the contrary, in my own case certainly, much knowledge and much hard thought, I know, had preceded the events. Nevertheless at the time of action it was and could have been used only in an intuitive way (not deliberately and consciously).

The point is well illustrated by the following: A friend of mine, a man of high intellectual attainments, of scientific training, and having conspicuously an incisive, logical type of mind, once said to me as we were playing golf: "Barnard, there is a place for brains in golf, but they must be used before you start the swing. If they are used during the action, it is invariably ruined."

However, I do not mean to suggest to you that for this reason my presentation of the case is worthless. In my interpretation now of what I was then doing, what I then thought, why I said what I did, why I interpreted the action of others as I did, it is to be borne in mind that I had been involved in many situations more or less similar, had directly or indirectly observed others in such situations, and between periods of critical action had studied and thought much about human behavior. This, together with the sequence of events, gives grounds for the probability that, in many respects at least, my present analysis is correct. It remains true, however, in view of what I have said, that my presentation of the case in this lecture hall constitutes a case in itself. You now observe my social behavior in a situation in which you are participants, when the object of our attentions is events that have previously occurred.

This leads me to say, as a final word of introduction, that I have participated in this case now in three ways.

First, when the events to be described took place. At this time, the action was concrete, synthetic, responsive, intuitive, not logical or analytical. At that time my position was the center of the situation from my point of view. Everything else was environment. I acted in, reacted to, and acted on that environment.

Second, on the night following the events, I analyzed the case. This was for the purpose of guiding future action of myself or anyone else. This time not I but the others were the center of the situation. I was out of it. What did it mean? What would be the consequences? Who should deal with it? This is analysis directed not toward knowledge but toward further action, intended to condition future more or less intuitive behavior or to select the ground of action, the strategic locus of future events.

Third, I now participate in the case by the present analysis. This is intended for knowledge, not action. In it, I endeavor to use experience acquired internally in the case but to present it as a whole. I am neither the center of the action, as in my first contact with it, nor entirely out of it as in the second. In making this presentation, I draw not only upon experience, both general and specific to the case, but also on general social knowledge. Indeed, except to those who had had much similar experience, I should not be able to present the case usefully in the absence of a conceptual scheme that afforded language which you can understand. In other words, I shall use many of the terms of Pareto's general sociology and of Professor Henderson's introductory lectures of this course, with the meanings, so far as I know, which they have in their writings respectively, and with which I assume you are well acquainted.

* * * * *

In the fall of 1931, being on various grounds much interested in unemployment and the need for relief, I accepted appointment by the Governor as State Director of Emergency Relief in New Jersey. I helped draft the necessary legislation and then organized the state's activity in the relief problem. In this position I was to a considerable extent the policy-making as well as the administrative authority. Hence, I gave much thought to the subject, acquired wide knowledge of conditions and of relief needs, and for about eighteen months was in responsible control of the work. Having other affairs requiring my attention, I then resigned. Governor A. Harry Moore many times generously expressed appreciation publicly. The legislature voted unanimous thanks for my services. There was no scandal, then or afterwards. Public attitudes were favorable. My service was without compensation. I was the head of a large corporation.

These statements are highly personal. I make them because I am asked to present a case as in a clinic, for educational or scientific purposes. If you bear this in mind you will find the personal references less offensive or annoying. The present point is to establish certain properties of myself as a person in the situation to be described. Note that the properties are of two classes: (1) The attitudes, knowledge, and abilities possessed by me; these, of course, have a bearing on my behavior. (2) Reputational properties — position, corporation standing (a social asset or liability, depending), volunteer worker, probably well-to-do or wealthy at least from standpoint of the jobless, without scandal, favorably treated by the public and political authorities after the job was done.

These two kinds of properties of persons are essential factors in every social situation. I shall refer to myself later and will also give you some of the properties of other participants in the case. Observe here, however, that the more constant elements of one's own conduct are the properties of the first class — character, knowledge, experience, skill, etc., and that the more variable elements are the reputational properties of the second class since they are ascribed by *other* persons. Being the more variable properties, i.e., being different for each situation, they are often conveniently regarded as the more important. People must react to what they *think* or *believe* you are. The distinction is of great importance both in personal careers and in concrete sociology.

In March 1935 a new governor and a new legislature decided to revise the general organization of the relief work. They provided that the general control and responsibility should be placed in a new board of ten persons. I was requested to serve as a member and was appointed. I was thereupon elected its chairman. It then appeared desirable that I should temporarily also serve as the executive head of the relief organization. At that time, due to many causes, the morale of the organization was low, and its work in some sections not well done. Financial difficulties were always pressing, and some confusion due to participation by the federal government was experienced.

Among the localities in which the work was not well handled was Trenton. For many reasons from the beginning in 1931 it had been weak. It was in 1935 in charge of a county director of estimable character and agreeable personal traits, but not strong enough for so difficult a task, and subject to interference as well as ill-informed criticism.

One result of this situation was that the unemployed in Trenton became organized in about eighteen districts each of which had a leader. This group of leaders demanded by letter to present their grievances in person to the Relief Council. Such a meeting was declined by the council with instructions to me as their chairman and also as state director of the work to meet these leaders. I appointed for the meeting a certain Tuesday when I could conveniently be in Trenton, Tuesday being the regular meeting day of the council.

On the day in question a mass meeting of the unemployed was held in some assembly hall. After it the crowd followed their leaders to the old Post Office Building, then used for relief organization work, where the council met, and where I was to meet the leaders in the office of our county director. This crowd was so large that it filled the streets adjacent to the building. It probably numbered not less than 2000 persons, and possibly was much larger. It had moved from its indoor meeting place to support its leaders in the negotiations. Its mood was happy, not belligerent, and as the conference began it was engaged in singing popular songs.

At this meeting eighteen leaders represented the unemployed. For the Relief Administration were the county director and myself. This disparity in numbers was intentional. The leaders had requested to meet with the entire relief council. Under many conditions, when there are no acute issues and there is no asperity, meetings between relatively large groups may be advantageous in facilitating understanding of points of view, in removing adverse misconceptions as to personalities, and in promoting the exchange of information. Where the issues are acute, the attitudes hostile, or misunderstanding is exaggerated, and especially when there is tension, it is desirable that numbers be reduced to a minimum, and the larger the number on one side, the smaller the number should be made on the other; for under such conditions misunderstandings are intensified by large numbers, and there are likely to be confusion and personal recriminations accompanying high feeling and a lack of control in the groups as a whole. In this situation there was one other reason for limiting the representatives of the Administration, which I shall explain in connection with the description of a second meeting later.

The decision was, it now appears, clearly wise; for the presence of the great crowd on the street, even though at first orderly and singing popular songs in pleasant mood, created a state of tension, under which neither I, nor my associate, nor any of the leaders could behave as we or they would under more usual conditions. The variations in the conditions which I call "states of tension" are among the more important variables pertinent to the behavior of groups. The quotation from Thucydides given in one of the introductory lectures of this course may be understood as saying that when there is a certain state of tension, called revolutionary conditions, the behavior of many men is utterly contrary to that which is normally observed in them.[3] I would define a state of social

[3] The quotation is as follows: "And revolution brought upon the cities of Hellas many terrible calamities, such as have been and always will be while human nature remains the same. . . . When troubles had once begun in the cities, those who followed carried the revolutionary spirit further and further and determined to outdo the report of all who had preceded them by the ingenuity of their enterprises and the atrocity of their revenges. The meaning of words had no longer the same relation to things but was changed by them as they thought proper. Reckless daring was thought to be loyal courage; prudent delay was the excuse of a coward; moderation was the disguise of unmanly weakness; to know everything was to do nothing. Frantic energy was the true quality of a man. . . . The lover of violence was always trusted, and his opponent suspected. He who succeeded in a plot was deemed knowing, but a still greater master in craft was he who detected one. On the other hand, he who plotted from the first to have nothing to do with plots was a breaker-up of parties and a poltroon who was afraid of the enemy. . . ."

The reader will be interested to compare this ancient comment with the

tension as one in which the attention of the individuals in the social situation is concentrated upon the *uncertainties* of their future personal status as affected by the events transpiring. Probably its subjective effect is to make the strategy of personal position the governor of behavior and hence to distort normal behavior both intellectually and emotionally, with reference to the subject matter of negotiation. Its most apparent effects are usually, I think, to increase the cohesiveness within the opposing groups and to extend the remoteness between them. Under such conditions, it is perhaps clear that the leader or spokesman for each side, if there be one, as the first objective must allay the tension, if constructive solution of differences is sought. Where there are wide differences in the position, prestige, power, and authority between the two sides the minimum of representatives of the side in the superior position reduces the tension, for physically, morally, and strategically in such situations there is strength in numbers, and superiority of position is counterbalanced by inferiority in numbers.

None of the leaders of the unemployed were known to me. Also, I had little specific knowledge of the conditions to which

---

following recent statement about the behavior of the Communists in France just before and after the beginning of World War II:

"The Communists at the works said that it was a purely imperialist war, that Daladier and Chamberlain were just as much enemies of the people as Hitler, and that the duty of the proletariat was to fight against its enemies at home, instead of serving as gun-fodder for their purposes. Put into practice, that would mean to surrender France to Hitler and the French working class to the Gestapo. But if you said so to a member of the C.P., you were a lackey of the bourgeoisie and a traitor. Half a year ago they had said exactly the contrary; they had issued fiery proclamations, urging the entire French nation, workers and bosses, to unite for the fight against the Nazi, and if you said anything critical about it, you were a Gestapo agent and a traitor. It was impossible to argue with Communists, they had a different party line every six months, and they were so fanaticized that they genuinely forgot what the last one had been; and if you reminded them, you were a Trotskist *provocateur* and a traitor." (Arthur Koestler, *Scum of the Earth*, 1941.)

they would refer or their recent history. In appearance, with one or two exceptions, they were large and powerful men. Most of them were badly dressed. Several showed effects of worry, malnutrition, and desperation. Due to their dress and appearance, I underestimated their intelligence, experience, and previous social status, as will appear later, but without unfortunate results. In manner and language, though occasionally excited and emotional, they were coherent; and they were respectful to me, in the sense of proper behavior between gentlemen, but not in the sense of subservience to my position. This favorably affected my own behavior.

I began the conference by having the county director present each man to me and I shook hands and talked with each of them. This was habitual behavior on my part, and not consciously designed. It deserves mention because it is a procedure often not followed under such circumstances and because of its bearing on the subsequent behavior. I then asked the men to tell me their story. I shall state later, in connection with a second meeting, the grievances they had to present.

While the conference was going on, the crowd outside was singing and was generally in order. Then, suddenly, shouts were heard, the singing stopped, and it was evident that something important was occurring. All members of the conference rushed to the windows. Below we saw police clubs flying, women trampled, men knocked down. It was clear that it was a bad and dangerous affair. It also seemed to me a disaster in unemployment relief and for the negotiations I was conducting. It was obviously impossible to continue the conference without a considerable recess until the extreme tension could be reduced.

Fortunately, the attitude of the leaders was one of sympathy for the crowd as again suffering from misunderstanding and official obtuseness and regret that their followers had come at all. They were, rather to my surprise, not hostile or bellicose;

and it was they who suggested that the conference be postponed. I set the same day of the following week, and suggested that they arrange in some way to reduce their members to about eight instead of eighteen, it being obvious that without a recognized leader, I could not negotiate with so many participants. This they agreed to do, and departed.

An hour later I left the building. The police thought it advisable to provide me a motorcycle escort which I declined as unnecessary. I mention it to indicate that all concerned, including myself, were in that state I have called extreme tension.

During the ensuing week, trials in the municipal courts took place. I had requested indirectly that the least possible punishment be given to the five or six under arrest. The newspaper comment was *hostile* to the unemployed. I had anticipated this and I feared it would make still more difficult the task ahead of me. What I desired most was to avoid all causes of tension so far as possible.

This ends the first half of my story. Though necessary for the background for the events to follow, it calls for only one observation of general character not already made. This concerns the motive of the crowd (not the leaders). This was, in my opinion, primarily that of action — of doing something. You will recall that one of Pareto's classes of residues [4] is en-

---

[4] "Residue" is a term used by Pareto to denote the sentiments that largely govern behavior, as manifested by the more persistent or less variable elements in what men say (and otherwise do also, as actually treated by him). It roughly means "motive," as most people appear to use the word, though Pareto thought he was deriving his "residues" by new methods. His classification of residues is elaborate, was not satisfactory to him, and is certainly not comprehensive. His six main classes of residues are as follows:

   I. Instinct for Combinations.
      This refers to the desire for putting things together, for invention, for exploring, to be clever in making new combinations of things.
   II. Group Persistences.
      This refers to the preferences for keeping things together that

titled: "the need of action to express sentiments." To this "need for action" I give a much more important place than Pareto. It is, I think, an almost universal though variable necessity of human beings, and one that is inadequately noticed both by men of affairs and by social scientists.[5]

---

have once been associated or combined, i.e., to the conservative sentiments.

   III. The need of Expressing Sentiments by External Acts (Activity-Self-Expression).
   IV. Residues connected with Sociality.
   V. Integrity of the Individual and his appurtenances.
   VI. The Sex Residue.

Pareto, who was dealing almost entirely with grand or very large societies, made little use in his book of any except the first two classes of residues. This is the occasion for the comment given on page 76.

[5] The need for action to which I refer is a fundamental physiological need related at least to circulation of the blood. I developed this point at considerable length in correspondence with Dr. Henderson, emphasizing that it has much to do with social action including acts of aggression, recreation, political behavior, and especially a very substantial amount of economic behavior. Dr. Henderson accepted my position in this matter and incorporated much of my material on it in his introductory lectures, as follows:

   Mr. Barnard points out that, while Pareto takes account of the need to manifest sentiments by actions and of the need to do something in an emergency, the need of action in general, the need to do something in general, is overlooked. In Mr. Barnard's opinion, this need is one of the principal forces determining the form of human societies. He says:

   "Children at all ages and especially when very young manifest this instinct. The contortionist and manipulative efforts of boys when alone and not aware of being observed are instances. The inability of most persons to remain seated; or their tendency to pace the floor, or to wander aimlessly about, or to play with watch chains, etc., are other simple cases. The avidity with which they embrace opportunities to 'do something' for no purpose, and entirely alone, is often observed.

   "Obvious as I think all this is, its significance for social science seems to me to be missed. For example, I am convinced that a large part of purely commercial transactions arise not out of economic considerations in any accepted sense but from the necessity of 'doing something.' People buy things they don't want — to 'do something.' They sell — to 'do something.' They build, speculate, trade — to 'do something.' They

Now the difficulties of finding opportunities for useful or legitimate action are substantial, especially among unimaginative persons, so that a breakdown of habitual channels of activity is a serious restriction or penalty to them. The unemployed as a class suffer especially from this. Attending a mass meeting, congregating at the place of our conference, singing songs, were more than all else a result of the need of "doing something." Although certain "foreign" agitators were undoubtedly at work, the behavior of the crowd was an innocent expression of a fundamental human need, notwithstanding that the conditions and the results were dangerous.

---

cover all this sincerely enough by rationalizations. Nevertheless, I believe anyone observing himself or others with this clue in mind will find ample confirmation, not only in the economic, but in every other field, probably including that of scientific investigation."

Bagehot expressed almost the same opinion: *The Works of Walter Bagehot,* Vol. IV, pp. 566–567, Hartford, Conn. 1889.

"Even in commerce, which is now the main occupation of mankind, and one in which there is a ready test of success and failure wanting in many higher pursuits, the same disposition to excessive action is very apparent to careful observers. Part of every mania is caused by the impossibility to get people to confine themselves to the amount of business for which their capital is sufficient, and in which they can engage safely. In some degree, of course, this is caused by the wish to get rich; but in a considerable degree too by the mere love of activity. There is a greater propensity to action in such men than they have the means of gratifying: operations with their own capital will only occupy four hours of the day, and they wish to be active and to be industrious for eight hours, and so they are ruined; if they could only have sat idle the other four hours, they would have been rich men."

Earlier, Bagehot cities a remark attributed to Pascal (*ibid.,* p. 564) "that most of the evils of life arose from 'man's being unable to sit still in a room.'"

In Mr. Barnard's view I concur, believing that it is important to include action of a type that extends far back phylogenetically in the analysis of residues. The problem of introducing this kind of residue into the classification is one of convenience. I suggest that the most promising procedure is to expand the definition of the instinct of combinations so as to include what Mr. Barnard would call the instinct for pure action.

On the Tuesday following these events, I had my second and final conference. There were eight representatives of the unemployed. We met in a small room around a table. I had determined after consideration that I would alone represent the Administration. I now believe that I had diagnosed the case as one in which the instincts of personal integrity — or self-respect — would be the dominating sentiments of the men with whom I would deal. I shall discuss this a little later. If this diagnosis were correct, the most desirable approach would be for me to meet them single-handed. The reason for this is that, when there is great disparity of position, rank, prestige, authority, in all of which respects I was far superior to these men, there is an initial fear or assumption by the inferior or subordinate that his personality, his position, his self-respect, will be or may be injured. I have myself experienced this feeling, which is often painfully uncontrollable, as no doubt have all of you. It is obvious that when the ratio is eight to one, however, this fear is allayed. Meeting the men alone was an expression of confidence in them as well as in the merits of my position and attitude; for the man who is alone under such conditions is in an exceedingly exposed and dangerous situation. He is far outnumbered in a physical sense in the event of disorder. He is at a serious disadvantage in any subsequent factual presentation — one memory against eight. He is verbally subject to attack from, and may have to defend himself against, eight different points of view. He submits himself to the possibility of misrepresentation and misquotation subsequently, when it may be his word against eight. Hence for me to meet them alone was something of an initial guarantee that no advantage of position was sought or would be taken. This was not only reassuring to those who were naturally fearful for their integrity, but it was positively complimentary and definitely recognized the personalities involved. I, therefore, took a dangerous course on the assumption that the diagnosis already

stated was correct and in the belief that I must win a correct
solution in order to prevent the spread of the movement and
the demoralization of the relief organization of the entire
State. I could not permit a prolonged and protracted public
controversy without injury to all concerned.

I must now refer to the personal properties of myself — in
the reputational aspects — which I have already stated. Both
my corporate position and my official position in the Relief
Administration were handicaps, in the sense that they tended
to make the men fear my incapacity, because of "remoteness,"
to understand their position, and to make them dread a lack
of consideration of themselves as individuals. The fact that
my previous service had been successful from a public and
political standpoint, that I was not a politician or professional
office holder, that I received no remuneration for my services,
and that no scandal or charges had ever been made, was an
inestimable negative advantage. I use "negative" in this sense:
I think it possible that none of these men knew any of these
things, or if they did know them were not consciously affected
thereby. If, however, in any of the respects named, the facts
had been reversed, then the fears of the men would have been
greatly increased and their suspicions aroused, for they would
certainly have known about such facts. An unfavorable reputation under inflamed conditions is a serious limitation for a
person in the situation in which I then was, and would have
radically altered my behavior and that of the others. For
example, I should probably have not dared to meet with them
alone.

It will now be useful to state briefly the character of the
men with whom I met. One of them I knew about. He was
a professional socialist agitator who had "made trouble" in
other areas among relief recipients in previous years. He was
intelligent, a good talker, well informed, on the whole reasonably well behaved. He did not dominate the others, who

were quite independent of him. Personal integrity was not a dominating but a secondary instinct with him — my original diagnosis was wrong as to him. I will state what his dominating sentiments were later. Of the others, one had been an auditor or accountant, the remainder (six) mechanics. All of them had earned fifty dollars per week or more in normal times, and half of them had owned their homes, although they had then all been lost by foreclosure. All were intelligent, generally good American citizens, and independent and courageous men.

Note that all of these men, except the professional agitator, had recently suffered violent injury to their personal integrities — their respect of themselves. This is inevitably an almost universal effect of prolonged inability to secure employment among those accustomed to work; and it reaches its apex in the necessity of accepting relief with the humiliating scrutiny of personal affairs this involves. In many the effect of this experience is to destroy interest, ambition, self-reliance, and to produce the appearance at least of indifference or of servility. But in men such as were in this conference, the instinct of self-respect, self-defense, personal integrity, was still strong, but raw and tender.

It was this upon which I had placed most reliance in my diagnosis, as evidenced by my behavior. I did not think that group persistences — in the form of adherence to radical doctrine, the class war, or organization solidarity — or the direct interests in relief were the points of attack or rather those to which I should adjust my behavior.

The first stage of the conference consisted in the recital of grievances, demands, criticisms. It lasted for two hours, during which I said little, except to ask questions or to inject an occasional comment. It confirmed my diagnosis. I could have myself expanded the list of complaints to ten times what they presented. With few exceptions the complaints were either trivial or related to past history no longer relevant to the existing conditions. As a whole they were utterly inadequate to explain or justify the organization of the relief recipients, their mass meeting, or the time and effort of the representatives, some of whom could certainly have employed themselves to better advantage materially in the endeavor to obtain jobs or create places for themselves.

What these men wanted was opportunity for self-expression and recognition. Their organization gave them one opportunity, our conference another. To have dismissed the grievances as trivial, however, would have been to destroy the opportunity that was literally more important to these personalities than more or less food for themselves or families. It is important for you to know that men often cannot talk about what they most want even when they are conscious of it. They could not say either to me or even to each other "I am starving to be recognized as a man, as a citizen, as a part of the community." To do so would itself destroy self-respect and would be futile as well. In this case, as in countless others, men talk and fight about what they do not want, because they must talk about something, and they even convince themselves that they believe what they say. Dr. Mayo [6] said to me once, as perhaps he has said to you, "I do not longer ask what men mean by what they say." I ask "Why do they say it?" And many, if not all, men of affairs do this intuitively as to those matters in which they are most skillful, although they frequently, if not usually, take statements literally in matters in which they are not skillful, or in which their emotions are overly powerful.

This is so important a matter that I repeat here the principal complaints, so that you may be sure of it.

[6] Dr. Elton Mayo, Professor in the Harvard Graduate School of Business Administration, who presented a case or cases in this course and who contributed much to the introductory lectures.

One was that six or eight months previously (under a different administration) a man was required to work in freezing weather in a ditch without proper shoes. Had it been unavoidable he would not have been outraged. He was a victim of stupidity and knew it. He brought it up because he did not know how to bring up his real present troubles.

Another complaint was that no drugs could be obtained without a doctor's prescription for which the Administration paid $1.50. It was a waste of money, they thought, where aspirin, for example, was all that was needed, and the money had better be put into larger food allowances.

A third was that a supervisor of relief was driving a Buick car, new, while these men were fed on a few cents a day. The offense disappeared when it was learned that it was a private car, not furnished by the Administration.

A fourth was that relief workers were rude, superior, too inquisitive, too discriminatory, played favorites. This was probably true in part, but not enough to be of general importance.

A fifth and real point was that men who worked (work relief) got *cash* (for food allowances only) with a bonus as against those who would not work, who received relief only in *food orders* without the bonus. This not only served to induce those unwilling to work to do so, but gave a certain disciplinary power to supervisors of work, since the discharge of a man put him in the non-cash category. This was sometimes abused.

A major point was that the allowances were insufficient. (At that time the food allowance in Trenton was about 6 cents per meal per person.) This was true; it was the most important point, but little was made of it.

Another was that mortgage interest and taxes were not paid by the Administration. This was chiefly a grievance against the depression rather than the Relief Administration and was so recognized; but a half hour's talk about it permitted much self-expression.

After about two hours of this, it seemed to me time to get into action. All the requirements of personal integrity (self-expression, self-respect) had been met so far as this kind of discussion could do it, and to continue would have produced false sensitiveness, exaggerated egos, a hypochondriac self-pity, which is the danger of recognizing personality by obvious direct appeal. It was now or never to test whether the diagnosis was correct, and whether the treatment was suitable. So I made the following speech:

Well, boys, I think I know what is in your minds and what you are complaining about. I think you have been moderate. I could kick about much more than you have. What I will do about it is this: What ought to be done either in the way of correction of faults or increases of allowances, I will do if I can, because they ought to be done. That is the only reason I and many others are in this work — to give you the most aid that we legitimately can. I think some improvements can be made. But you cannot have relief in cash if you do not work, because the council and many others believe that would merely favor the good-for-nothing loafers against the interest of you and many others. Moreover, some of the things you want we probably cannot do because we cannot get enough money, and we must be sure to make what we have go all the way round. That is in your interest more than in that of anyone else. There are some other things I would like to do, but will fail in doing, because we can only employ ordinary human beings in the Administration. You will not always be treated either as you wish to be or as we would like to have you. If you were doing this work, you would be subject to the same criticisms you level at others.

That is as far as I can, or anybody ought to, go. But one thing I want to make clear. I'll be God damned if I will do anything for you on the basis that you ought to have it just because you want it, or because you organize mass meetings, or what you will.[7] I'll do my best to do what

---

[7] In my judgment, confirmed by others whose opinion I respect, it is as a general rule exceedingly bad practice for one in a superior position to swear at or in the presence of those of subordinate or inferior status, even though the latter have no objection to oaths and even though they know that the

ought to be done, but I won't give you a nickel on any other basis. In saying this, you know it isn't my money, and it means nothing to me personally. My position is based more on your own interest than on anything else. For the kind of behavior which you have been exhibiting is alienating from you the very people upon whom you or I depend to get the money for relief, and I assure you there are many who object to giving it now.

This was said with plenty of emphasis. They were fighting words and presented the position on which I was prepared to fight. And they brought a fighting reaction. One big fellow jumped up with a flushed face to announce that it was only a section of high-hat people with money who objected, and who didn't know what it was all about anyway, so far as he was concerned.

I suppose my effort was to bring him and the others to a middle and sane position. When a boy, I had been told that if a horse is frightened by something on one side, whip him on the other. Some extreme statement might work here. So I said: "That's where you're wrong, and you have too many troubles to be wrong about this one. The well-to-do have lost plenty and are grumbling much about taxes and this or that, and lots of them have lost their nerve. But they're not the people who are opposed to you." And then I continued with a statement which I believed to be true, but which I did not think five intelligent persons in the state would accept at that time. It was: "The people who are most opposed to you and whom you and I must pay most attention to are those near-

---

superior is accustomed to cursing. I have known very few men who could do it without adverse reactions on their influence. I suppose the reason is that whatever lowers the dignity of a superior position makes it more difficult to accept difference of position. Also, where a single organization is involved in which the superior position is symbolic of the whole organization, the prestige of the latter is thought to be injured. In the present case, an exception, the oath was deliberate and accompanied by hard pounding of the table.

est to you — those just one jump ahead of the bread line." [8]
To my utter amazement the socialist agitator said: "He's dead
right. That's the crowd we have to fear."

The tension had been so great and the confirmation so un-
expected that for a moment I was baffled. But the battle was
over at that point. We had succeeded in uniting in a common
view.

After another hour's discussion, one of the men said: "I
think we better leave it in Mr. Barnard's hands. He understands our language and what it's all about, and is out to do
the best he can for us. I think we would be smart to let him
work it out for us."

As I look back on it, I do not think I had ever before made
a purely personal accomplishment the equal of this, or that I

---

[8] (Original note, 1938.) This point may deserve elucidation here, since it
is certainly not obvious even yet. In 1935 the principal concrete evidence of
the correctness of this opinion was the hostility of farmers toward relief.
Most of the farmers were themselves in bad condition and in many cases had
need for relief. As to other classes, chiefly in the cities, the indirect taxation
for relief financing, and the borrowing of money for it, produced the illusion
that relief was not a burden to the class nearest, but not on relief. In New
Jersey at the time about 15% of the population were dependent on relief. I esti-
mated that 15% were also just one step removed from relief. In this class,
fear of being forced on relief, and scorn for some relief recipients, produced
a lack of sympathy. When direct taxes (sales taxes) were proposed, this attitude at once became pronounced.

The intervention of the Federal Government in relief has had for one important effect the prevention of the development of active hostility. Its method
of financing both by deficits, and largely income and indirect taxation, has
not impinged on the lower income groups, and it has seemed to them as if
relief were paid for by the intangible thing called "business" and the well-to-
do. If the Federal Government had not in the later years chiefly financed
relief, the states would have had to resort to heavy direct taxation, and the
hostility of the lower classes (economically) would have then been apparent.
This has been observed in the smaller towns and the rural sections where relief
(except W.P.A.) has been returned to local operation. There is very little
given in many such places.

Other federal policies, unnecessary to mention here, have also had an important bearing on tolerance toward the unemployed.

am likely to equal it again. Yet I was not impressed at the time — an indication of how intuitive and responsive my whole behavior was. In fact I did not report on it to the relief council and I have never told anyone about it in detail until now, except a friend last week who asked what I would present to you. It seemed then merely another hard day and a tough job that was back of me.

A few months later, I resigned and returned to private business. But there was no further trouble for many months and then in a different connection. A year or so later this group (joined by many others) occupied the assembly chamber in the capitol for a number of days in the attempt to force certain legislative action.

To complete the analysis, I should now make a few final observations. The first of them relates to the order of importance of Pareto's classes of residues (see footnote, pp. 65–66). You will recall that although he gives six classes, he uses the first two, the Instinct of Combinations and the Group Persistences, almost exclusively in his discussion of general social systems. It may be that this emphasis will prove correct for the analysis of the behavior of large collectivities, but I believe this emphasis is not correct as respects small societies or organizations. There is no necessary inconsistency in these two views. In the case I have presented you have noted that my own conduct was based upon the diagnosis that the Instinct of Personal Integrity (Pareto's Class V) was the primary sentiment in the situation. This proved, I think, to be correct except as to one man — the socialist agitator. In his case, I believe that the Instinct of Combinations was the dominant factor. The principal reason for this belief is that he so quickly and avidly confirmed my judgment that the enemies of the unemployed were those nearest their position. If either his personal egotistic instincts or his group persistences (socialist doctrines) had been dominant, he probably would not have agreed or at least would not have stated his agreement. In these small and concrete social situations, I suggest that either the need of action, instincts of sociability, or those of personal integrity, especially the latter, are primary, and other sentiments secondary.

A second observation is that economic considerations or interests were negligible in the case presented. They were not wholly absent, of course; and one who observed only what the men *said* would have perhaps reached a contrary opinion. The chief economic factor in the situation related to my own behavior, since I had strongly in mind the financial limitations of the relief organization and the problems of public finance and taxation. But even in my own behavior, I should describe the economic factors as limiting or conditioning elements rather than determinants of concrete action. The importance of this observation is great. In innumerable instances I have observed, even when the subject matter of social interaction is economic — for example in business transactions — the behavior manifests chiefly non-economic sentiments. Since the language used is so largely of economic character, this is not obvious. But this language is largely derivation,[9] rationalization, and frequently approaches ritualistic symbolism — for example in certain habitual expressions in meetings of boards of directors. The behavior of purchasers and of employees is generally accompanied by expressions of economic interests. Very frequently, however, these interests are quite subordinate and may even be negligible. This will not appear on the surface and is concealed by the fact that some kind of economic transaction or result is usually the most tangible effect of the social interaction involved. This leads often to interpretation of situations in exclusively economic terms, whereas the concrete behavior was governed by the need of action, the love of

[9] Pareto's term for non-logical or illogical statements and arguments.

combinations, the desire to build up personal integrity (desire of prestige, status). At the present time it appears to me that a large part of social discord and friction is due to the illusion that economic interests govern behavior almost exclusively in business, industrial, and political situations.

Again, I would note the essentially emotional, responsive, intuitive, non-logical, and relatively non-intellectual character of the behavior in the case presented. An observer might easily be deluded about this, since a large part of the action consisted in sentences, argument, which appeared rational at least in part. Such non-rational factors as the order of speaking, the tone of voice, the emphasis, the time and manner of interruptions, the facial expressions, the gestures, the silences, which are essential aspects of the concrete situation, are quite unconscious to the actor and are *felt* rather than observed by other participants. This is all concrete and too rapid and interlocking to permit analysis even if the participants were competent to analyze such complex phenomena, or even if there were an acceptable science for the purpose, which is not yet the case. This is typical of most social situations.

Finally, in conjunction with what I have just said, observe the necessarily progressive character of diagnosis in such situations. An experienced man of affairs has said of it to me: "That was a situation in which it would be impossible for anyone to say in advance what he would do." A preliminary diagnosis could at best be provisional. Making such a diagnosis, one starts treatment, as it were, and observes reactions in further symptoms and signs, which confirm, modify, or destroy the diagnosis. It is comparatively rare, and then only when one can generalize from a number of apparently similar situations, that a firm diagnosis can be adopted prior to the action itself. This is why most men of experience will not formulate a diagnosis or prescribe their own action in advance, even to themselves (except when desirable for purposes of argument in *another* situation). To do so, is to give evidence of misunderstanding of the nature of social action. It is necessarily nonlogical in most instances and is for this reason usually unpredictable in the specific case, although undoubtedly subject to some uniformities and probabilities in a large number of cases.

IV

THE NATURE OF LEADERSHIP [1]

INTRODUCTION

LEADERSHIP has been the subject of an extraordinary amount of dogmatically stated nonsense. Some, it is true, has been enunciated by observers who have had no experience themselves in coordinating and directing the activities of others; but much of it has come from men of ample experience, often of established reputations as leaders. As to the latter, we may assume that they know how to do well what they do not know how to describe or explain. At any rate, I have found it difficult not to magnify superficial aspects and catchphrases of the subject to the status of fundamental propositions, generalized beyond all possibility of useful application, and fostering misunderstanding.

Seeking to avoid such errors, I shall not tell you what leadership is or even how to determine when it is present; for I do not know how to do so. Indeed, I shall venture to assert that probably no one else knows. These statements may seem strange and extreme, but I hope to convince you that they are not ex-

---

[1] Copyright, 1940, by Chester I. Barnard. This paper contains the substance of two similar addresses given on January 24, 1940 before the Chemical Reserve Officers of the Second Corps Area, U. S. A., under Colonel A. Gibson, C. W. S., U. S. Army, then Chemical Officer of the Area, and on March 9, 1940, before Professor Philip Cabot's Week End Conference of Business Executives at the Harvard Graduate School of Business Administration. On both occasions the speaker submitted to questions at considerable length. The substance of the important questions and answers is also incorporated in this paper, which was privately printed for the author in 1940 and was reprinted by permission in *Human Factors in Management,* edited by Schuyler Hoslett, Park College Press, 1946.

pressions of false modesty or of ill-considered judgment. At any rate, what I intend to discuss is *the problem of understanding the nature of leadership.*

The need for wide consideration of this subject was most forcibly impressed upon me by two observations, made on a single occasion, which revealed the extent of public misunderstanding of it. Some time ago I attended a large joint conference of laymen and members of the faculty of an important university to consider the subject of educational preparation for leadership. At this meeting my first observation was that *leadership* was confused with *preeminence* or *extraordinary usefulness* both by speakers and by audience. In their view a leading writer, artist, pianist, mathematician, or scientist, exemplifies leadership substantially as does an executive or leader of an organization. No one appeared to be aware of the double meaning of "leadership" and its implications for the discussion of the subject of preparing "leaders." Among the meanings of the verb "to lead" we may say that one is: "to excel, to be in advance, to be preeminent"; and another is "to guide others, to govern their activities, to be head of an organization or some part of it, to hold command." I think the distinction between these meanings is rather easy to see. Most individuals matured in a well-organized effort recognize it as a matter of course, so that it may be difficult for many who from long experience thoroughly understand the distinction to believe such a confusion common. I fear that it is common, however, and is making cooperation and adequate organization increasingly difficult.

My second observation at this meeting, further evidence of the same fact, was this: During the period of open discussion, a well-known engineer protested the subjection of engineers to supervision or management by those not engineers. The superiority of engineers in nearly all respects, especially in intellect, training, and science, was implied. Though the audience was not one of engineers, it expressed derision generally at the absurd state of affairs portrayed. Could there have been a more striking proof of the misconception of the subject these several hundred earnest, intelligent, educated people were discussing — how better to prepare people to be leaders?

These observations show the importance of public discussion of the problem. Mere knowledge of how to solve it would not be sufficient. Often, in similar matters, when a solution is available it will not be accepted unless the problem itself is either acknowledged as such by reliance upon a responsible authority or is recognized and accepted by agreement and understanding. Otherwise a correct solution is merely "one man's idea, a little queer"; and a "solution" is something that cannot be made effective because it *will* not be used. This seems often not to be adequately taken into account in the discussion of social and organization "remedies."

Now it seems to me evident that the problem of leadership, like some others which now obsess us, is not yet suitably formulated. For this reason, if for no other, it is not generally understood. This needs emphasis because within our own organizations we usually do not experience much difficulty on this account; for we already have an approximately common understanding or sense, coming from long interconnected experience, which is workably adequate. Such an understanding is a substitute, and a superior one, for abstract knowledge of the matter — at least for any I imagine being available for a long time. But outside these circles of intimate experiential knowledge, understanding fails, even among leaders.

Not only misunderstanding but positive need for leaders warrants our attention to this subject. The large scale integrations of our present societies — the great nations, the immense organizations of war and peace, of culture and religion — make the needs of leadership relatively greater and its functions more complex than heretofore, so that the necessary proportion of leaders to the population has greatly increased. In other words, the "overhead" of any organization or society clearly tends to expand more rapidly than its size. Moreover, technology and specialization make the arts of leadership even more complex than consideration of size alone would indicate. These facts suggest that scarcity of leaders of requisite quality may already limit the possibility of stable cooperation in our societies.

I think we may agree, then, that public misunderstanding and misinformation, and the need for provision of more adequate leadership, both urge our effort to understand the nature of leadership. My present attempt to contribute to this end ought chiefly, I think, to make evident the present obscurity of the subject and the complexity of the functions and conditions involved in it. This method of approach will surely try our patience and may be discouraging to some; but we shall be wise in this matter not to give answers before we have found out what are the questions. The attitude that I think we may best have has been admirably stated by T. S. Eliot:

> The fact that a problem will certainly take a long time to solve, and that it will demand the attention of many minds for several generations, is no justification for postponing the study. And, in times of emergency, it may prove in the long run that the problems we have postponed or ignored, rather than those we have failed to attack successfully, will return to plague us. Our difficulties of the moment must always be dealt with somehow; but our permanent difficulties are difficulties of every moment.[2]

In the light of these preliminary remarks it may be well for me to state the meaning of the word "leadership." As I use it herein it refers to the quality of the behavior of individuals whereby they guide people or their activities in organized effort. This is its primary significance. Organized effort takes

[2] T. S. Eliot: *The Idea of a Christian Society,* Harcourt, Brace & Co., New York, 1940.

place, however, in systems of cooperation which often include property or plants. When this is so, the activities coordinated relate to, or are connected with, the property or plant, and the two are not separate. Hence, the management or administration of such properties, as distinguished from the command or supervision of personnel, is also included as a secondary aspect of leadership.

Whatever leadership is, I shall now make the much over-simplified statement that it depends upon three things — (1) the individual, (2) the followers, and (3) the conditions. We shall agree at once, no doubt; but unless we are careful, I suspect that within an hour we shall be talking of the qualities, capacities, talents, and personalities of leaders as if the individual were the exclusive component of leadership. Therefore, let me emphasize the interdependence by restating it in quasi-mathematical language, thus: Leadership appears to be a function of at least three complex variables — the individual, the group of followers, the conditions.

Now the points to note here are two. First, these are variables obviously within wide limits, so that leadership may in practice mean an almost infinite number of possible combinations. Second, if we are to have a good understanding of leadership we shall need a good understanding of individuals, of organizations, and of conditions, and of their interrelationships so far as relevant to our topic. Do we have that now? I am sure we do not. Yet I fear this may be thought an extreme theoretical view unless I give some demonstration of its correctness, and at the same time give some idea of how we might at least approach some better practical understanding.

In undertaking this, I shall depart from the scheme of the three variables and proceed along more everyday lines. To present my suggestions of possibilities as to the nature of leadership, I shall give the following: (I) A general description of what leaders have to do in four sectors of leadership behavior; (II) Thoughts concerning certain differences of conditions of leadership; (III) Some remarks about the active personal qualities of leaders; (IV) A few notes on the problem of the development of leaders; and (V) Observations about the selection of leaders.

I. Four Sectors of Leadership Behavior

Leaders lead. This implies activity, and suggests the obvious question "What is it that they have to do?" Now, I must confess that heretofore on the few occasions when I have been asked: "What do you *do?*" I have been unable to reply intelligibly. Yet I shall attempt here to say generally what leaders do, dividing their work under four topics, which for present purposes will be sufficient. The topics I shall use are: The Determination of Objectives; The Manipulation of Means; The Control of the Instrumentality of Action; and The Stimulation of Coordinated Action.

Unfortunately it is necessary to discuss these topics separately. This is misleading unless it is remembered that, except in special cases or when specially organized, these kinds of action are not separate but closely interrelated, interdependent, and often overlapping or simultaneous. Therein lies one reason why it is so difficult for a leader to say what he does or to avoid misrepresenting himself. He does not know how to untangle his acts in a way suitable for verbal expression. His business is leading, not explaining his own behavior, at which, though sometimes voluble, he is usually rather inept, as we doubtless all are. Indeed, as I shall show later, it is *impossible* for him to be aware of this behavior in the sense necessary to explain it except very generally on the basis of his observations of others as well as of himself.

THE DETERMINATION OF OBJECTIVES

Let us consider the first sector of behavior.

An obvious function of a leader is to know and say what to do, what not to do, where to go, and when to stop, with reference to the general purpose or objective of the undertaking in which he is engaged. Such a statement appears to exhaust the ideas of many individuals as to a leader's *raison d'être*. But if they are able to observe the operations closely, it often disconcerts them to note that many things a leader tells others to do were suggested to him by the very people he leads. Unless he is very dynamic — too dynamic, full of his own ideas — or pompous or Napoleonic, this sometimes gives the impression that he is a rather stupid fellow, an arbitrary functionary, a mere channel of communication, and a filcher of ideas. In a measure this is correct. He has to be stupid enough to listen a great deal, he certainly must arbitrate to maintain order, and he has to be at times a mere center of communication. If he used only his own ideas he would be somewhat like a one-man orchestra, rather than a good conductor, who is a very high type of leader.

However, one thing should make us cautious about drawing false conclusions from this description. It is that experience has shown it to be difficult to secure leaders who are able to be properly stupid, to function arbitrarily, to be effective channels of communication, and to steal the right ideas, in such ways that they still retain followers. I do not pretend to be able to explain this very well. It seems to be connected with knowing whom to believe, with accepting the right suggestions, with selecting appropriate occasions and times. It also seems to be so related to conditions that a good leader in one field is not necessarily good in others, and not equally good under all circumstances. But at any rate, to say what to do and when, requires an understanding of a great many things "on the whole," "taking everything into account," in their relations to some purpose or intention or result — an understanding that leads to distinguishing effectively between the important and the unimportant *in the particular concrete situation,* between what can and what cannot be done, between what will probably succeed and what will probably not, between what will weaken cooperation and what will increase it.

THE SECOND SECTOR — THE MANIPULATION OF MEANS

There is undoubtedly an important difference between the kind of effort we have just considered and the direction of detailed activities that are parts of technical procedures and technological[8] operations as the subsidiary means and instruments of accomplishing specific objectives already determined. Sometimes an exceptional leader can effectively guide technical operations in which he has no special competence, whereas those of high competence are often not successful leaders. I shall not attempt a general explanation of these facts; but on the whole we may regard leadership without technical competence as increasingly exceptional, unless for the most general work. Usually leaders, even though not extraordinarily expert, appear to have an understanding of the technological or technical work which they guide, particularly in its relation to the activities and situations with which they deal. In fact, we usually assume that a leader will have considerable knowledge and experience in the specifically technical aspects of the work he directs. I need not say much about this, for it seems to me that at present we overestimate the importance of technical skill and competence and undervalue, or even exclude, the less tangible and less obvious factors in leadership.

Nevertheless, the technical and technological factors in leadership not only constitute a variable of great importance, but they introduce serious difficulties, which should be mentioned, especially in respect to (1) the development of types of leaders, and to (2) the limitations these technical factors place upon

[8] Throughout I use "technological" exclusively to refer to conditions of physical technology — plants, machines, chemical processes; and "technical" to refer either to systems of procedure in accounting, management, etc., or in a more general sense to cover both ideas.

the "mobility" of the leaders in an organization or society, and also (3) because of the restrictive effect of technical study and experience on the *general* or "social" development of individuals.

(1) It is almost a matter of course that leadership "material" will be inducted into organization through some particular technical channel. Such channels are now highly specialized. When the course has been run, the man has been trained for leadership only with respect to a narrow range of activities. Otherwise he is untrained, and hence (2) the mobility of leadership resources may be seriously reduced because it is difficult to use a good leader of one narrow field in another field or in more general work — a fact which I suppose is now well recognized at least in all large organizations of industry and government and education. This difficulty, which is real, has become exaggerated in our minds, so that in my opinion we all — leaders and followers — tend to overlook superior leaders who at the moment may be lacking particular technical qualifications.

(3) Concerning the third difficulty — the effect of specialization upon the individual — it is only necessary to note that while men are concentrating upon techniques, machines, processes, and abstract knowledge, *they are necessarily diverted to a considerable extent from experience with men, organizations, and the social situations, the distinctive fields of application of leadership ability.* Thus at the most impressionable period they become so well grounded in "mechanical" attitudes toward non-human resources and processes that they transfer these attitudes, then and later, toward men also.

The technical sector of leadership behavior is not a new thing in the world, but its importance has greatly increased. By technology and specialization we have accomplished much; but the resulting complexity of leadership functions and the restriction of the development and supply of general leaders seems to me one of the important problems of our times.

THE THIRD SECTOR — THE INSTRUMENTALITY OF ACTION

Leadership obviously relates to the coordination of certain efforts of people. There is little coordination or cooperation without leadership, and leadership implies cooperation. Coordinated efforts constitute organization. *An organization is the instrumentality of action so far as leaders are concerned, and it is the indispensable instrumentality.* Many promising men never comprehend this because of early emphasis upon plants, structures, techniques, and abstract institutions, especially legal institutions such as the law of corporations.

The primary efforts of leaders need to be directed to the maintenance and guidance of organizations as whole systems of activities. I believe this to be the most distinctive and characteristic sector of leadership behavior, but it is the least obvious and least understood. Since most of the acts which constitute organization have a specific function which superficially is independent of the maintenance of organization — for example, the accomplishment of specific tasks of the organization — it may not be observed that such acts at the same time also constitute organization and that this, not the technical and instrumental, is the primary aspect of such acts from the viewpoint of leadership. Probably most leaders are not ordinarily conscious of this, though intuitively they are governed by it. For any act done in such a way as to disrupt cooperation destroys the capacity of organization. Thus the leader has to guide all in such a way as to preserve organization as the instrumentality of action.[4]

Up to the present time, leaders have understood organization

---

[4] The conception of the nature of organization — as a system of coordinated *activities* — involved in this paragraph is carefully developed and defended in *The Functions,* chapter vii, "The Theory of Formal Organization," and is made more explicit in the article "Comments on the Job of an Executive." See the preliminary note of the title page.

chiefly in an intuitive and experiential way. The properties, limitations, and processes of organization as systems of coordinated action have been little known in abstraction from concrete activities and situations; but the persistence and effectiveness of many organizations are evidence that leaders know how to behave with respect to them. On the other hand, we know that many very able, intelligent, and learned persons have neither understanding nor correct intuitions about concrete organizations.

THE FOURTH SECTOR — THE STIMULATION OF COORDINATED ACTION

To repeat a commonplace, it is one thing to say what should be done, and quite another to get it done. A potential act lies outside organization, and it is one task of leaders to change potentiality into the stuff of action. In other words, one important kind of thing that leaders do is to induce people to convert abilities into coordinated effort, thereby maintaining an organization while simultaneously getting its work done. I need hardly say that this kind of activity of leaders is sometimes the most striking aspect of what they do. In a broad sense this is the business of persuasion. Nor need I say that the sorts of acts or behavior by which executives "persuade" to coordinated action are innumerable. They vary from providing the example in "going over the top," or calm poise inspiring confidence, or quiet commands in tense moments, to fervid oratory, or flattery, or promises to reward in money, prestige, position, glory, or to threats and coercion. Why do they vary? Some obvious differences of combination in leaders, in followers, in organizations, in technology, in objectives, in conditions, will occur to you. But the effective combinations are often so subtle and so involved in the personalities of both leaders and followers that to be self-conscious about them, or for others to examine them when in process, would disrupt them.

*   *   *

My chief purpose in this brief account of four sectors of leadership behavior has been to indicate how interconnected and interdependent they are and to suggest how great is the variation in what "leadership" means specifically, depending upon the relative importance of the kinds of behavior required.

II. The Conditions of Leadership

Already it has been necessary to allude at least by implication to differences in conditions of leadership, such for example as are involved in the degrees and kinds of technological operations. I shall now confine the discussion to differences of conditions of another sort, relating to the degree of tension of the action of leaders, followers, or both. It will be sufficient to consider only the two extremes.

The first is that which we may call stable conditions. These may be complex and of very large scale; but they are comparatively free from violent changes or extreme uncertainties of *unusual* character or implying important hazards. The behavior of leaders under such conditions may be calm, deliberate, reflective, and anticipatory of future contingencies. Leadership then is lacking in the dramatic characteristics often observed at the other extreme, and this is one of its difficulties; for its function of persuasion must be carried on without the aid of emotional drives and of obvious necessities and against the indifference often accompanying lack of danger, excitement, and sentiment. Stable conditions call for self-restraint, deliberation, and refinement of technique, qualities that some men who are good leaders under tense conditions are unable to develop.

The other extreme is that of great instability, uncertainty, speed, intense action, great risks, important stakes, life and death issues. Here leaders must have physical or moral courage, decisiveness, inventiveness, initiative, even audacity; but I believe we tend to overstate the qualities required for this extreme, due to its dramatic aspects and because the outcome of action is more easily judged.

This is enough to suggest that differences of conditions of this type, that is, differences in tension, are important factors in leadership behavior. It should be apparent that we could expect only rarely to find men equally adapted to both extremes, and that quite different types of leaders are to be expected for this reason. Yet it is obvious that emergencies may be encountered in any kind of cooperative effort, and that leaders have to be adapted to function under wide ranges of conditions. Indeed, intermittent periods of severe stress are the rule in navigation, in military organizations, in some kinds of public utility work, in political activity, to cite a few examples in which particular types of *flexibility* are necessary to continuous leadership. It may be apparent here, as perhaps it was in considering the sectors of leadership behavior, that the practical problem in selecting specific leaders would be to ascertain the *balance of qualities* most probably adapted to the conditions or to the variations of conditions.

III. The Active Qualities of Leaders

I have already stated why I do not think it useful to discuss leadership exclusively in personal terms. Leaders, I think, are made quite as much by conditions and by organizations and followers as by any qualities and propensities which they themselves have. Indeed, in this connection, I should put much more emphasis upon the character of organizations than upon individuals. But this is not the common opinion; and I certainly should not fail to discuss that quite variable component, the individual.

I shall list and discuss briefly five fundamental qualities or characteristics of those who are leaders, in their order of importance as regarded for very *general* purposes. Probably I shall not include qualities that some think essential. I would not quarrel about what may be only a difference in names or emphasis. Perhaps, also, there will be disagreement about the order I have chosen. This I shall mildly defend, my chief purpose being to correct for a current exaggerated and false emphasis. The list follows: (i) Vitality and Endurance; (ii) Decisiveness; (iii) Persuasiveness; (iv) Responsibility; and (v) Intellectual Capacity.

I. VITALITY AND ENDURANCE

We should not confuse these qualities with good health. There are many people of good health who have little or moderate vitality — energy, alertness, spring, vigilance, dynamic qualities — or endurance. Conversely, there are some who have poor health and even suffer much who at least have great endurance. Generally, it seems to me, vitality and endurance are fundamental qualities of leadership, though they may wane before leadership capacity does.

Notwithstanding the exceptions, these qualities are important for several reasons. The first is that they both promote and permit the unremitting acquirement of exceptional experience and knowledge which in general underlies extraordinary personal capacity for leadership.

The second is that vitality is usually an element in personal attractiveness or force which is a great aid to persuasiveness. It is sometimes even a compelling characteristic. Thus few can be unaffected by the violent energy with which Mussolini throws his arm in the Fascist salute, or by the vehemence of Hitler's speech, or by the strenuous life of Theodore Roosevelt. Similarly, we are impressed by the endurance of Franklin D. Roosevelt in campaign.

The third reason for the importance of vitality and endurance is that leadership often involves prolonged periods of work and extreme tension without relief, when failure to endure may mean permanent inability to lead. To maintain confidence depends partly on uninterrupted leadership.

II. DECISIVENESS

I shall be unable to discuss here precisely what decision is or involves as a process, but I regard it as the element of critical importance in all leadership, and I believe that all formal organization depends upon it. Ability to make decisions is the characteristic of leaders I think most to be noted. It depends upon a propensity or willingness to decide and a capacity to do so. I neglect almost entirely the appearance or mannerism of being decisive, which seems often to be a harmful characteristic, at least frequently misleading, usually implying an improper understanding and use of authority, and undermining confidence. Leadership requires making actual appropriate decisions and only such as are warranted.

For present purposes decisiveness needs to be considered in both its positive and negative aspects. Positively, decision is necessary to get the right things done at the right time and to prevent erroneous action. Negatively, failure to decide undoubtedly creates an exceedingly destructive condition in organized effort. For delay either to direct or to approve or disapprove, that is, mere suspense, checks the decisiveness of others, introduces indecisiveness or lethargy throughout the whole process of cooperation, and thus restricts experience, experiment, and adaptation to changing conditions.

III. PERSUASIVENESS

The fundamental importance of persuasiveness I have already mentioned. Here I refer to the ability in the individual to persuade, and the propensity to do so. Just what these qualities are defies description; but without them all other qualities may become ineffective. These other qualities seem to be involved, yet not to be equivalent. In addition, persuasiveness appears often to involve or utilize talents, such as that of effective public speaking or of exposition or special physical skills or even extraordinary physique, and many others. The relation of specific talents to leadership we cannot usefully consider further here. But at least we may say that persuasiveness involves a *sense* or understanding of the point of view, the interests, and the conditions of those to be persuaded.

IV. RESPONSIBILITY

I shall define responsibility as an emotional condition that gives an individual a sense of acute dissatisfaction because of failure to do what he feels he is morally bound to do or because of doing what he thinks he is morally bound not to do, in particular concrete situations.[5] Such dissatisfaction he will avoid; and therefore his behavior, if he is "responsible" and if his beliefs or sense of what is right are known, can be approximately relied upon. That this stability of behavior is important to leadership from several points of view will be recognized without difficulty; but it is especially so from that of those who follow. Capricious and irresponsible leadership is rarely successful.

V. INTELLECTUAL CAPACITY

I have intentionally relegated "brains" to the fifth place. I thereby still make it important, but nevertheless subsidiary to physical capacity, decisiveness, persuasiveness, and responsibility. Many find this hard to believe, for leaders especially seem to me frequently to be inordinately proud of their intellectual abilities, whatever they may be, rather than of their more important or effective qualities.

---

[5] An extended exposition and illustration of this definition are given in *The Functions* in chapter xvii, "The Nature of Executive Responsibility."

This attitude may be partly due to a confusion between pre-eminence and leadership — an instance of which I gave in my introduction — and partly to the high social status now given to intellect, to which I shall refer later. Disagreement as to the subordinate place to which I here assign intellect may also be partly due to a matter of definition; for I think we usually confuse *acquirement* by intellectual processes with responsive, habitual, intuitive *expression* or *application* of what has been acquired, which I take to involve processes largely non-intellectual.

However, I believe sensitiveness about our intellects is often due especially to the fact that the part of behavior *of which we are most conscious* is at least largely intellectual, whereas much of our most effective behavior, such as reflects vitality, decisiveness, and responsibility, is largely matter-of-course, unconscious, responsive, and on the whole has to be so to be effective. Self-consciousness in these respects would at least often check their force, speed, or accuracy. Moreover, leaders, like others, are for the most part unaware of their most effective faculties in actual behavior, for they cannot see themselves as others do.

This last point is so important both in theory and in practical administration that I think it worth further consideration here. The point is easy to prove, but its implications are difficult to explain. For the proof we may take, as an example, speaking and its accompanying gestures. It is well known that no one hears his own voice as it sounds to others chiefly because much of the vibrations of the speaker's voice are conducted within the structure and passages of the head. I believe that an individual without previous experience rarely recognizes his own voice from a good reproduction. Some are greatly surprised and often displeased at hearing such a reproduction for the first time. Obviously, too, an individual cannot see his own demeanor or many of his movements. Yet in all our relations to others the use of voice and gestures is of first importance and both are effectively controlled to a considerable extent so as to accomplish specific reactions in listeners. If we cannot hear and see ourselves as others do, how can we accomplish such control of our behavior?

I think the explanation may be as follows: We learn to correlate our own speech and action, as we hear and feel them, with certain effects upon others. We are only approximately successful, and some are much more so than others. Listeners and observers, on the other hand, learn to correlate the entirely different thing, our observable behavior, with our meanings and intentions. This is also only approximate, and is done more successfully by some than by others. Since leadership primarily involves the guidance of the conduct of others, in general, leaders need to be more effective than others both in conveying meanings and intentions and in receiving them.

These fundamental processes are certainly not to any great extent intellectual. We all know that the capacity to understand the logical significance of sentences, even when written or printed, is limited, and that repeatedly we understand by the manner of speaking. We can with some success teach by logical processes what to do in the operation of a machine or process, though even here we know that often to state a direction correctly in language is to mislead, whereas an incorrect statement especially with appropriate gesture or facial expression may well convey the precise meaning. But to teach by logical exposition how to behave with other people is a slow process of limited effectiveness at best. This is why I think it will be widely observed that good leaders seldom undertake to tell followers *how* to behave, though they tell what should be done, and will properly criticize the manner of its doing *afterward*. Whereas inferior leaders often fail by trying, as it were, to tell others how to live their lives.

THE LIMITATIONS OF INTELLECTUALS

Whatever may be the explanation of our strong predilection for our intellectual attainments, it is difficult to evade the emphasis I have placed on other qualities in leadership. We all know persons in and out of practical affairs of superior intellects and intellectual accomplishments who do not work well as leaders. In matters of *leadership*, for example, they prove to be irresponsible (absent-minded, non-punctual), non-decisive (ultra-judicial, see so many sides they can never make up their minds), non-persuasive (a little "queer," not interested in people). Moreover, we can observe that intellectual capacity rarely rises above physiological disabilities in active life, that the utmost perspicacity is useless for leadership if it does not decide issues, that persuasive processes must take full account of the irrational by which all are largely governed, that responsibility is a moral or emotional condition.

THE IMPORTANCE OF INTELLECTUAL CAPACITIES

Intellectual abilities of high order may achieve preeminent usefulness. They are sometimes an important element in leadership but not sufficient to maintain it. However, as a differential factor — that is, other qualities being granted and adequate — intellectual capacity is of unquestioned importance, and especially so in the age in which complex techniques and elaborate technologies are among the conditions of leadership. Leaders of the future, in my opinion, will generally need to be intellectually competent. However, the main point, which I wish greatly to emphasize, is that intellectual competency is *not* a substitute, at least in an important degree, for the other essential qualities of leadership.

SOME EFFECTS OF EXAGGERATED INTELLECTUALISM

Though it may be unpleasant to some, I have laid stress upon my opinion in this matter for two principal reasons. The first is that under present trends an excessive emphasis is placed upon intellectual (and pseudo-intellectual) qualifications by responsible "selecting" authorities, which artificially limits the supply of leaders. The same excessive emphasis upon the intellectual is made by followers who are intellectuals. Thus it is often difficult for them (experts and professionals of many kinds) who have no administrative capacity (or interest) to follow even extraordinary leaders. This is a form of conceit frequently accompanied by exhibitions of temperament and disruptiveness, and by false, ruthless, and irresponsible professions of individualism and freedom, especially professional and academic freedom. All of this tends to a limitation of the supply of competent leaders, because it discourages men from undertaking the work of leadership, and it restricts their effectiveness.

My second reason is that a general condition amounting to intellectual snobbishness, it seems to me, has a great deal to do with industrial unrest. I see this in the propensity of educated people, whatever their economic status or social position, to underestimate the intelligence and other important personal qualities of workmen; in the tendency of some supervisors, quite honestly and sincerely, to blame failure to lack of brains in subordinates instead of to the stupidity of instructions; in the assumption of some men that "pure bunk" dressed up in "high brow" jargon is effective in dealing with people; in the excessive popularity of white-collar occupations; in the desire of so many intellectuals to tell others how to eat, save money, dress, marry, raise families, take care of their own interests. These are symptoms of attitudes and it is the latter, not the symptoms, which are important. They cause division of interest artificially and lack of sympathetic understanding that are destructive of cooperation and cannot be corrected by mere "measures of good will."

I am well aware that there are differences in the intellectual capacities of men and know that such differences are important, especially as respects the ability to acquire knowledge and understanding by study in those matters which can only be learned in this way. Nevertheless, after a fairly long experience in dealing with many classes of men and women individually and collectively, the destructive attitudes I am attacking seem to me to be unwarranted by anything I know about intellect, education, or leadership. Intellectual superiority is an obtrusive thing which even intellectuals dislike in others except as they *voluntarily* give it their respect.

OUR IGNORANCE OF THE QUALITIES OF LEADERSHIP

After this long digression it may have been forgotten, though observed, that in this discussion of personal qualifications I have failed, with one exception, to define my terms. Though in a general way I am confident that my meaning is understood, greater precision of meaning seems quite impossible, at least without extended space, and is not needed here. Indeed, a significant fact to emphasize is that neither in science nor in practical affairs has there yet been attained a degree of understanding of these qualities now vaguely described which permits much clear definition even for special purposes.

It is worthwhile to illustrate this with reference to "decisiveness." The making of decisions is one of the most common of the events of which we are conscious both in ourselves and others. We believe that many decisions are momentous either to ourselves, to our enterprises, or to our society. We may agree that those incapable of making *any* decisions are at least morons if not insane. We are aware that to make decisions is a leading function of executives. We also know that decisions are made collectively, as in committees, boards, legislatures, juries, and that such work is one of the most characteristic features of our social life. Yet decisive behavior, as contrasted with responsive behavior, seems to have received little attention in the psychologies,[6] in the literature of logical operations, in sociology, and seldom in economics. Moreover, in business I rarely hear appraisals of men in terms of their capacity for decision, except when they fail apparently for lack of ability to decide. It seems clear that we know so little of this quality or process that we do not discuss it as such, though "decision," "decisive," and "decisiveness" are words frequently on our lips.

I am aware, as I said earlier, that I have omitted several qualifications of leadership which commonly stated. In my intention, they are all comprehended in the five I have named or in some combination or derivation of them. Three omitted qualifications are great favorites: "honesty" ("character"), "courage," and "initiative." They may be added; but for myself I find them words which depend for their meaning in the specific case upon the *situation,* not merely the individual, either as interpreted by the actor or leader or others, and that his

[6] While writing this sentence I have taken off the shelf at random more than a dozen books on psychology and social psychology. In only two is "decision" indexed (Lewin: *Principles of Topological Psychology* and Guthrie: *The Psychology of Human Conflict*) and in both cases the citations are few and quite secondary. Of course, perhaps all of the elements of the decisive processes may be covered in all these books, though from my recollection of them I doubt it. The fact is that one of the most conspicuous factors in common current observable behavior simply has not been recognized as such, notwithstanding that decision is the culmination of whatever we mean by "free will," "will," "voluntary," "determined" (in some meanings). The situation recalls what one psychologist has said of others, though in another connection: "All such explanations fail to explain why we think that A is A. For, even when the psychologists told us that A really was B, we stubbornly persisted in calling it A and not as B . . . For in the long run it has proved to be more profitable to accept an A as an A and explain it as such . . ." (K. Koffka, *Gestalt Psychology,* Harcourt, Brace and Co., Inc., 1935, p. 179.)

interpretation will often differ from the interpretations made by different observers.

In any case, the important point is that the qualifications of leadership, however discriminated and however named, are interacting and interdependent. We do not assemble them as we would the ingredients of a compound, yet we may suppose that different combinations of qualities produce quite different kinds of leaders, and that the qualities and their combinations change with experience and with conditions.

IV. The Development of Leaders

I think I have now shown that my profession of ignorance of this subject and my doubts with respect to the knowledge of others concerning it were both justified. Yet I recognize that however lacking in knowledge we may be, we nevertheless endeavor in our educational systems and at least in the larger organizations to increase the number of available leaders and their competence. It might be suggested that I should say something on this aspect of the subject in the light of my earlier remarks. I shall confine myself briefly to development methods and, in the next section, to the processes of selection.

Concerning the development of leaders, I shall in this section discuss the following topics: (i) Training; (ii) Balance and Perspective; and (iii) Experience.

I. TRAINING

As I understand it, the only qualification for leadership that is subject to specific preparatory training by formal processes is the intellectual, including therein the inculcation of general and special knowledge. My opinion as to the relative importance and status of intellectual qualities has already been stated to the effect that such qualities are increasingly necessary to effective leadership in technical and technological fields and also in large-scale organizations where complexity and the remoteness of concrete activities call for capacity in the handling of abstract material. The latter are the conditions in which leadership also usually involves management of extensive cooperative systems as well as of organizations.

Nevertheless, I believe it should be recognized that intellectual preparation by itself tends to check propensities indispensable to leadership. For example, study and reflection on abstract facts do not promote decisiveness and often seem to have the opposite effect. Analysis, which broadly is characteristic of intellectual processes especially in the early stages of education and experience, is the reverse of the process of combining elements, of the treatment of them as whole systems involved in concrete decisive action, for instance in persuasion. As a result of intellectual training many prefer to recognize only what has been stated or is susceptible of statement and to disregard what has not been stated or is not susceptible of statement. The emphasis upon abstract facts characteristic now of the "more intelligent" and dominant classes of our population has its results, in innumerable instances, in the "fallacy of misplaced concreteness," the confusion of the fact with the thing and of *an aspect* with an indescribable whole, in the disregard of the interdependence of the known and the unknown.

An example of this or of its general effects may be found in the excessive emphasis upon knowledge as against skill in nearly all fields except sports and individual artistic performance. Yet but a moment's reflection is needed to acknowledge that many of the noteworthy efforts of scientist, teacher, lawyer, physician, architect, engineer, clergyman — to take professions in which intellectual discipline and experience are indispensable — are expressions not of intellect but of skills, the effective behavior by which the appropriate adjustment to the infinite complexity of the concrete is accomplished. Indeed, we repeatedly confess the point in our practical emphasis upon experience, if not upon intuition, in every profession.

Nowhere is the emphasis upon fact to the exclusion of the thing to which it relates more harmful, it seems to me, than in the human side of industrial relations. We may think of employees as mechanics, clerks, laborers, or as members of an organization, but to lead requires to *feel* them as embodying a thousand emotions and relationships with others and with the physical environment, of which for the most part we can have no knowledge.

The dilemma which this state of affairs presents is, I think, concealed by the increasing extent to which prestige and status based on education are the basis of general social and industrial discrimination. I mean by this that a certain intellectual and educational status has become important, to the relative disregard of other qualifications, in getting a job, or at least a job generally regarded as desirable or distinctive. We can hardly help believing that an attitude is useful to society as a whole if we find that same attitude socially imposed upon us as individuals.[7]

II. BALANCE AND PERSPECTIVE

It may be thought that changes in curricula might be sufficient to correct for the tendency toward distortion of judgment which I have described. This may be possible in the future but not yet. So far as I know there is not developed the basic material for such changes, and it is unlikely that there will be unless my view of this problem, assuming it to be correct, should be accepted widely. But at best I should expect such studies only to offset the prejudices inculcated, possibly excepting the humanities, by higher education.

[7] An analogous problem is presented in "oversaving" theories of depressions, in which it is asserted that it is possible for a society as a whole to oversave, whereas the desire to save is commendable as to individuals.

Hence, for the present, it seems to me that balance, perspective, and proportion in the senses relevant to leadership are to be acquired almost exclusively from responsible experience in leading.

III. EXPERIENCE

In speaking of experience, it will be well to avoid the common error of regarding it as primarily a matter of repetition through a period of time. When experience is merely repetition of action, it is better called practice to acquire patterns of behavior. It is often convenient as a rough approximation to speak of hours, days, months, or years of experience, but we know that some men learn slowly, others quickly. Moreover, the possibility of learning depends upon activity. If nothing happens, little can be learned. Significant experience is secured largely by adapting one's self to varieties of conditions and by acquiring the sense of the appropriate in variations of action.

The acquirement of experience under modern conditions presents us with another dilemma; for the refined specialization and the technical complexity through which men are now introduced into the world of affairs give limited opportunity for general experience in leadership. The most "natural" opportunities at present formally available seem to me to be the small *general* business, political party work in communities, and perhaps to a less extent, labor union leadership. These are insufficient sources for the supply of general leaders. Hence, we need to develop the artificial methods of giving wide experience which are now attempted to some extent in large organizations.

The effect of technical work is so strongly opposed to the acquirement of experience in the arts of leadership that I cannot forbear to add a suggestion that encouragement should be given in gaining experience informally in "extracurricular" activities. In fact, though we can as yet apparently do little in a formal way to develop leaders, we can encourage potential leaders to develop themselves, to seek for themselves the occasions and opportunities when leadership is needed, to learn the ways of making themselves sought as leaders, to acquire experience in leading by doing it. I have myself been so encouraged and inspired in my youth and since then, as no doubt we all have, so that to give such encouragement seems to me an important private and social duty; but I believe whatever we do in this respect will be harmful if not done in full realization that *there is no substitute for the experience of recognizing and seizing opportunities, or for making one's own place unaided and against interference and obstacles;* for these kinds of ability are precisely those that followers expect in leaders.

V. Selection

Thus we have to recognize that leaders, almost blindly created by physiology, physical environments, social conditions, and experience, are now secured chiefly by selection, not by formal preparation. Our success is relative in the sense that we select as best we may of the quality that is presented but are little able to affect favorably that quality as a whole except as to the intellectual element. If this is a fact, it is admittedly difficult to observe, because to do so requires comparison of what we have with what we think we might have. Yet if we believe it to be a fact, it implies a precarious position; for the most perfect selection would not suffice to give adequate leadership if the supply of the "raw material" were of inferior quality, any more, for example, than the best selection among untutored electricians would be likely to afford an adequate supply of superior electrical engineers.

The test of the adequacy of leadership is the extent of coöperation, or lack of it, in relation to our ideals; and this is largely a matter of the disposition of followers. Even in this brief discussion it should be stated that in all formal organizations selection is made simultaneously by two authorities, the formal and the informal. That which is made by formal authority we may call appointment (or dismissal), that by the informal authority we may call acceptance [8] (or rejection). *Of the two, the informal authority is fundamental and controlling.* It lies in or consists of the willingness and ability of followers to follow.

To many who have struggled and worried regarding appointment or dismissal of leaders, and to whom the maintenance of formal authority is the very keystone of cooperation, order, and efficiency, what I say may seem absurd or even subversive. But we have all many times proved it correct. For has not our first question always been in effect "Can he lead and will they follow?" If our answer were "No!" would we not appoint at the peril of our own leadership? And when there has been failure of followers to follow, writhe as we would, were not our only recourses to change the leader or possibly to change the followers?

If it is thought that this doctrine is subversive, this may be because it is thought to be what uninformed preachers of the vague thing called "industrial democracy" want, and we suppose they know less of leadership and organization than even we do. But what they advocate and what we fear is the transfer of *formal* authority from leaders to voters, forgetting that the informal authority must finally determine, whatever be the nature of the formal authority. Indeed, this latter fact is the chief reason for our fear; for we recall the men who have been enthusiastically elected but never followed. As to most (but not all) leadership, *appointment* by responsible leaders

[8] Under some, usually small or local, situations leaders are acclaimed spontaneously and are induced or forced to lead by pressure of social opinion. There is often some element of this even in large and institutionalized organizations, chiefly expressed on the negative side, i.e., it is socially or organizationally not countenanced to quit leading or to refuse promotion, and loss of "caste" would be involved.

has proved, and I believe will continue to prove, more effective and more satisfactory to followers than any other formal process.[9] And the followers make the leader, though the latter also may affect and must guide the followers.

I turn now to the process of selection, by formal authority of appointment or dismissal. In the selective process we eliminate for positive disqualifications — bad health, lack of ability to decide, irresponsibility, lack of adequate intellectual or technical ability. Frequently this is all disregarded most conveniently by saying "lack of experience" when what we mean is "lack of successful experience." For although a few eliminations are made for positive disqualifications, the really important basis of selection is that of prior achievement. Since we know so little about the qualifications for leadership, this often proves a fallacious method, sometimes resulting in tragic errors and often in a great deal of foolish rationalization. Nevertheless, we must confess that the past record is the best basis of selection we have. Thirty years ago Mr. Theodore N. Vail, a great leader and organizer in his day, and then President of the American Telephone and Telegraph Company, said to me: "You never can tell what a man will do by what he has done; but it is the best guide you have." I believe this still to be true; but I do not think it is an adequate basis for selection of leaders for our society of the future.

If leadership depends, as I have said, upon the individual, the followers, and the conditions, there must be many failures that are not the result of original errors of selection. For men, followers, and conditions all change. We are prone to forget this and to condemn, perhaps because it imposes upon us one of the most serious problems in the selective process. Failure of leadership if not corrected by replacement means the checking of the experience and development of potential leaders. Hence

[9] My reasons are developed at length in the lecture, "The Dilemmas of Leadership in the Democratic Process," cited in the preliminary note.

the elimination of super-annuated, obsolete, and incompetent leaders is recognized as extremely important in most organizations, perhaps most systematically in the Army and Navy. But this process is extremely delicate; for though followers cannot follow those who cannot lead, those who have been superior leaders embody or personify the spirit of an organization and represent the aspirations of their followers. Crude dismissal at any level of organization destroys morale and ambition and thus does violence to organization itself. In all types of organizations I believe this often means retaining a leader in the interest of everyone concerned after he has passed the peak of his capacities and sometimes even when the latter have become inadequate. When this is a matter of favoritism there can be no good defense of it; but when it is a part of the process of *organizing leadership* involving the supplementing of incapacities by auxiliary leaders, it must be defended.

Here we are confronted with another problem of balance — another of the dilemmas of our subject. Who will say that we now know enough about it or are sufficiently successful with respect to it?

CONCLUSION

In this short study of one aspect of life, I have tried to emphasize the extent of our limitations and the importance of overcoming them, both from the standpoint of the effect of public blindness to the nature of the problem — which results so often in obstruction and in destructive criticism — and also from the standpoint of preparation to meet the future needs for leaders. These are ever increasing as the integrations of our societies grow larger, and as specialization and technological progress continue. Whether such an account is depressing, perhaps appalling, or is challenging and inspiring, will depend, I suppose, upon one's philosophy, outlook, or temperament.

It is in the nature of a leader's work that he should be a

realist and should recognize the need for action, even when the outcome cannot be foreseen, but also that he should be idealist and in the broadest sense pursue goals some of which can only be attained in a succeeding generation of leaders. Many leaders when they reach the apex of their powers have not long to go, and they press onward by paths the ends of which they will not themselves reach. In business, in education, in government, in religion, again and again, I see men who, I am sure, are dominated by this motive, though unexpressed, and by some queer twist of our present attitudes often disavowed.

Yet, "Old men plant trees." To neglect today for tomorrow surely reflects a treacherous sentimentalism; but to shape the present for the future by the surplus of thought and purpose which we now can muster seems the very expression of the idealism which underlies such social coherence as we presently achieve, and without this idealism we see no worthy meaning in our lives, our institutions, or our culture.

CONCEPTS OF ORGANIZATION[1]

THE purpose of this paper is to develop the concept of organization employed in *The Functions of the Executive,* to set forth the conceptual scheme employed therein, and to show its relation to the theory of organization. These are matters that have puzzled some readers who have found the treatment of them unacceptable or incomprehensible or impractical. I am ready to concede that this may be largely the fault of the exposition; but it is also in part attributable to some novelty in the conceptions employed of organization and of the commonly recognized elements such as authority, incentives, communication.

Before proceeding with specific topics, it may be helpful to explain what I found to be the essential problem in writing about organization — a problem that is still unsolved for those concerned with the exposition of organization and management or administration. When I began the preparation of a series of Lowell Institute Lectures on the functions of executives, it was my intention merely to give an orderly description of what executives do and how they work. I soon found, however, that I could do this only in terms relating to the structure and dynamic characteristics of organizations. Two difficulties in using such terms immediately appeared. The first was that they would not only be meaningless to those without experience in organizing and in directing organizations un-

---

[1] A revision of the major portion of an article entitled "Comments on the Job of the Executive" appearing in the *Harvard Business Review,* Spring, 1940. See the preface of the present volume, pp. v–vi.

less their meaning were carefully explained, but that these terms would also be almost as meaningless to those with such experience. This is due to the facts that different terms are used in different organizations for the same things, and that the same terms mean different things in different organizations. A review of the literature of organization, management, and administration reveals vagueness, ambiguity, and non-standard nomenclature.

An attempt to correct this situation by carefully defined terms and accurate description reveals the second difficulty. This is the lack of adequate concepts. Not merely the words but the ideas are vague, and those that are adequate for work-a-day purposes in concrete situations are not so for comparative and general purposes. Thus the exposition depended upon the selection and construction of concepts that would permit of a logically consistent treatment of the subject matter with the maximum of definiteness and the minimum of ambiguity. Scientific communication in this field awaits the development and acceptance of a set of concepts and a definite language. What I have done is merely a preliminary and incomplete construction, for testing by myself and others interested.

The need for the conceptualizing effort and its relation to the development of theory, I discuss later. But first I should discuss the central concept of organization.

I. The Relationship of Customers to Organization

The conception of organization at which I arrived in writing *The Functions of the Executive* was that of an integrated aggregate of actions and interactions having a continuity in time. Thus I rejected the concept of organization as comprising a rather definite group of people whose behavior is coordinated with reference to some explicit goal or goals. On the contrary, I included in organization the actions of investors, suppliers, and customers or clients. Thus the material of organization is personal services, i.e., actions contributing to its purposes. In stating what was required to elicit such services from individuals, however, it was convenient to make the application and to use the terms appropriate to the relationships of those contributors usually called employees or "members" of the organization. Thus I said (*The Functions,* p. 227):

The second function . . . is to promote the securing of the personal services that constitute the material of organizations. The work divides into two main divisions: (I) the bringing of persons into cooperative relationship with the organization; (II) the eliciting of the services after such persons have been brought into that relationship.

The methods and means by which those services are elicited are stated thus (p. 231):

As executive functions they may be distinguished as the maintenance of morale, the maintenance of the scheme of inducements, the maintenance of schemes of deterrents, supervision and control, inspection, education and training.

The failure to carry out this analysis in terms appropriate to customers, ordinarily thought of as having a quite different relationship to an organization than employees have, is occasion for confusion of the reader to whom it then appears that the author is confused. This makes clarification desirable. It will be attempted in two stages, as follows: (1) demonstration that an act of purchase by a customer is a part of the organization of the seller; (11) argument that the economy of incentives which was presented specifically in terms of employer-employee relationships applies equally to seller-buyer relationships.

I

1. When the acts of two or more individuals are cooperative, that is, systematically coordinated, the acts by my definition constitute an organization. Every such act is a component

simultaneously of two or more systems as determined by its functions. Thus every act of organization is also an act of some individual and is his contribution to the organization. When two or more organizations cooperate, the cooperative acts are simultaneously (1) of individuals, and either (2) of the organization contributing the act and (3) of the second organization participating, or (4) of a new complex organization embracing the two original organizations cooperating, or of all four. This simultaneous functioning of the cooperative act of an individual in two or more organization systems provides the interconnection which results in complex organizations (*The Functions,* pp. 111, 112). These statements are made explicit at the outset to forestall the natural reaction on first consideration that a duplication is inadvertently admitted.

This will seem to many, no doubt, a strange, artificial, unrealistic kind of thing chiefly because they will not realize that this is precisely the kind of thing they are working with in their minds in a rough-and-ready way all the time. Take, for instance, a *man* who is always changing, or a *corporation* of which the principal nearly constant attributes are its name and by-laws, or, to get farther toward the earth, take a *whirlpool.* This is a realistic thing to one who gets into it, and it seems real enough to anyone who watches it. When you use the name nearly everyone knows what you mean, and there is no other name commonly covering the same thing. But if asked what it is, I think you might have to say something like this:

A whirlpool is a *situation* in a body of water in which there are comparatively stable uniformities of relations between streams of molecules of water, moving with increasing rapidity spirally towards a center called a vortex, the level of which is depressed with reference to the level of the surrounding water. The movement of the streams of molecules is downward at the vortex. New molecules move into the situation as fast as old ones move out. The position of the whirlpool also may move as is easily seen by the movement of the vortex. If the molecules stop moving in this way, there is no whirlpool, because all there is to a whirlpool is streams of molecules of water moving in certain ways. And don't ask what a "stream" is.

Others will be puzzled at the idea that a single act can be called part of several organizations at the same time, yet we have no difficulty with the same or similar idea when we are used to it. For example, no one seems to have so much difficulty as I think he might with the idea that a man can be simultaneously a citizen of Massachusetts and a citizen of the United States, or that when he votes for a United States Senator he by a single act at once performs, as a citizen of the Commonwealth, a function of choosing a representative for the state and also elects, as a citizen of the United States, an official of the government of a nation. I had no difficulty in realizing when I signed a letter for the company this afternoon that it was an act of at least three systems: of my family, without which it is possible I should not have done it and which in any event uses most of the proceeds, of myself, for it was at least my muscles that did the work, and I probably should not have been available if I had disliked it enough or had been ill, and of the company, without which it is literally inconceivable that *this* act should have been performed.

To put the matter in reverse, you could not completely understand a specific act of a human being without knowing all the organizations in which the *act* functioned as a part. If this sounds "abstract" and "unrealistic," let me put it this way: you cannot deal effectively with people unless you can get their "point of view," which means knowing what "influences" govern their behavior. This is easily said but really almost impossible to *comprehend* without a *conception* which treats it as simpler than it is. This is the great function of a good conceptual scheme. It makes it possible to deal consciously and effectively with infinite complexity.

2. In a community all acts of individuals and of organizations are directly or indirectly interconnected and interdependent. Analogously all elements of the physical universe are said to be interconnected and interdependent. For convenience obviously necessary in some degree, we disregard the interconnections which we consider minor or trivial and distinguish those that are direct and that constitute stable systems or organizations, just as we do in the case of physical systems. Usually the organizations which are stable are those which are named or can be readily named. When two stable organizations cooperate, it is convenient to regard the cooperative acts as common to both organizations only, and not as creating a new and enlarged organization. The exception to this is where this interorganization cooperation is itself a stable system constituting a complex organization (*The Functions,* chapter viii). Such complex organizations are usually characterized by formal systems of communication and authority.

3. Among the simplest of organizations is the exchange of goods between two men, A and B. Perhaps we often fail to think of an exchange as cooperative, because emphasis is so much placed upon conflict of interest or bargaining in a hostile sense, conditions that may precede exchange; but a moment's reflection is sufficient to see that an exchange is based upon *agreement* to effect a *transaction,* a coordination of acts of the two parties, the acts being mutually dependent and interconnected. We should not be misled by the ephemeral character of this particular case. It is perhaps more short-lived than a microbe and may be dismissed as unimportant. But the aggregate of the relations between what is exchanged by such cooperation is the subject matter of economic science; and also the aggregate of such acts constitutes, at least in part, stable unit and complex organizations and is the subject of the study of cooperation.

In an exchange of goods, let us call the act of A, a, and of B, b. Then the organization involved in the exchange is $(a + b)$.[2]

4. More complex is the cooperation of an employer and an employee, A and C. Here an exchange is involved, as it was above between A and B, and a numerous series of cooperative acts of C is required and at least one (payment) by A. This creates a duration and stability of personal relationship between A and C, usually not present in the first case, A and B; but there is no other essential difference. Regardless of this personal relationship, the acts coordinated by agreement constitute the organization. Let us denominate by (a) the acts of A, within a given period of time, and indicate the number of acts by subscript, thus a_n, and similarly for C, c_n. The organization named (A-C) is then $(a_n + c_n)$.

5. Let now an exchange be made between (A-C) and B, an individual. This involves an additional act of (A-C), performed for it by say the individual A and an act of B. Then by definition we say (1) the organization (A-C) becomes $(a_{n+1} + c_n + b_1)$; and also we may say (2) that there is a new organization named (A-C)B, which would be expressed $[(a_{n+1} + c_n) + b_1]$. The latter we usually disregard as ephemeral.

6. Let B now engage an employee D whose acts we denote by d_n. The organization is called (B-D). If now an exchange (exactly the same as in paragraph 3 above) be made between (A-C) and (B-D), A and B performing the acts of exchange, we say that the organization (A-C) then consists of $(a_{n+1} + c_n + b_1)$, and that the organization (B-D) consists of $(b_{n+1} + d_n + a_1)$. There is also a new complex organization not named

[2] For purposes of simple illustration I am assuming that an exchange involves only one act of each party. At least two and usually many are required, a fact of no importance here.

which is expressed $(a_{n+1} + c_n + b_1) + (b_{n+1} + d_n + a_1)$ or $(a_{n+1} + b_{n+1} + c_n + d_n)$. For many purposes we disregard the latter organization.

7. These statements make more explicit the implications of the definition of organization given in chapter vi of *The Functions*. There is no equivocation about the matter; nor am I debating now the usefulness of the definition.

8. In the sense of ultimate analysis an organization is a composition of cooperative *acts*. It is convenient to deal with certain aggregates of such acts as named organizations and to classify them in various ways. Several I have listed in chapter viii, "Formal Organizations." The identification of particular organizations and their analytical classification will depend on the purpose or convenience to be served — usually what (superficially) the organization does, or who most stably contributes to it. Hence the X.Y.Z. Steel Co., or the Excelsior Department Store, or the Suburban Division. This emphasis upon some characteristic in discriminating and labeling organizations should not lead us to exclude some classes of cooperative acts. We may think of the department store as a group of employees, as a physical plant, as a stock of goods, but it nevertheless remains a *store* because of the cooperative acts of customers.

II

I now propose to apply to customers the methods of eliciting services from employees to demonstrate that as material of organization they are essentially alike. These methods, as previously quoted (p. 113), were the maintenance of morale, the maintenance of schemes of inducements, the maintenance of schemes of deterrents, supervision and control, inspection, education and training. I seek to show that in the fundamental sociology of business behavior the services of an employee and of a customer when making a purchase are equivalent elements, similar contributions to the *same* organization, and that every statement quoted above applies unequivocally to either employees and their cooperative acts or customers and their acts of purchase. It is customary to use different names in connection with the two categories of contributors to organization — employees and customers — such as "morale" as to employees and "goodwill" as to customers, but this is merely a matter of customary terminology that tends to conceal similarities without being based upon differences essential from the point of view of the theory of cooperation.

Of the statements quoted above, I now purpose *to apply every single item* to the customer relationship, showing what are the facts and also what are the words ordinarily used to describe them on the level of "realistic" and practical discourse, as follows:

(1) The bringing of customers into cooperative relationship; (2) the subsequent eliciting of services; (3) the maintenance of customer morale; (4) the maintenance of the scheme of inducements; (5) the maintenance of the scheme of deterrents; (6) supervision and control; (7) inspection; (8) education and training.

Establishing the Cooperative Relationship

It needs little exposition to show that whether the services of employees or of customers are in question, it is necessary to bring either into cooperative relationship before they can or will cooperate. (In both cases the techniques of advertising and salesmanship are employed, with persuasion as a major characteristic.) "Salesmanship" is not a word used with respect to active efforts to secure employees, "personnel work," "employment work," "recruiting," being the words used; but salesmanship is what it is. This is especially evident today when trying to secure skilled mechanics. It is an important aspect of recruiting "college material." It is the business of

getting people to look at what you have to offer as inducements and incentives for cooperation and of persuading them
to accept the offer. A confusion as to the nature of the functions may be due to the fact that we predominantly think of
employees as seeking jobs, rather than employers as seeking
employees, just as we predominantly think of sellers seeking
customers. In many, perhaps most, instances the buyers of
goods may be said to seek the seller, not the seller the buyer,
especially if we disregard the effect of advertising.

Eliciting the Acts of Cooperation

When once the cooperative relationship has been established,
the exchange that constitutes organization is to be elicited. The
exchange in one case (that of the employee) is services for
money, in the other (that of the customer) money for services
(the act of transferring goods or services). It hardly needs
discussion that it is one thing to get the employee on the pay
roll, and another to get the services. Similarly, it is one thing
to get the customer in the store, another to make the sale.

Maintenance of Customer "Morale"

The maintenance of morale among employees depends upon
attitudes, "fair treatment," working conditions, inducements,
and incentives. So does also the maintenance of morale — the
desire and willingness to cooperate, that is, to purchase — on
the part of customers. If it is attained, it is called "goodwill."
How much a part of the conditions of organization it is, is indicated by the fact that goodwill is often a (salable) asset of
the business enterprise. The techniques in both cases are iden-
tical or similar, the chief variations being due to time, place,
and degree of continuity of cooperation. Thus customers are
influenced by incentives (values, prices), by manner of treatment, by kind of persons with whom they must associate to
cooperate (quality of salespeople), the working conditions —

location, cleanliness, light, air, crowding, etc. — of merchandising. One needs to know little of business to see how important this is in business "policy."

Application of Inducements and Incentives to Customers

Surely it is easily recognized that the maintenance of a scheme of inducements is equally required and is of the same nature whether one refers to employees or to customers. The essence of both relationships is exchange. In both cases, economic goods are involved, and in both cases other inducements than those *recognized* in the economic exchange are present. Every one of the incentives I listed (*The Functions,* p. 142) is in general applicable equally to the customer and the employee relationship. Not all of them are important in any given situation of either kind. Usually only two or three will be so regarded in a given situation, and what these are will be a matter of the specific conditions in each case. However, as this may not be obvious, at the risk of being tedious I shall give examples for each incentive listed on the page cited, applied to the customer relationship:

a. Material inducements. This is obvious and is implicit in the definition of customer.

b. Personal non-material opportunities (*The Functions,* pp. 145–146), such as opportunities for distinction, prestige. Much appeal of banks, department stores, and specialty shops is that they afford opportunities for distinction and prestige to customers. It can hardly be doubted that this is an important element in many customer relationships.

c. Desirable physical conditions (of work, p. 146). It is necessary only to refer to air-conditioning, paneled walls, expensive fixtures, location, to see how important desirable physical conditions of purchasing are.

d. Ideal benefactions. It is only necessary to listen or to observe one's own conduct to know that loyalty to a purveyor is often an important basis of continuing customer relationships and that many successes, especially among smaller retailers, are based on deliberate conduct intended to promote and grant this kind of satisfaction.

e. Associational attractiveness. One would need only to know of the attention paid in many establishments to kind and quality of sales personnel, and the degree to which employees are retained because of the personal relationships between employee and customer, to recognize the importance of this incentive to customer cooperation.

f. Customary purchasing conditions and conformity to habitual practices are clearly an important element in goodwill. Great effort and expense are often made to avoid disturbing customary conditions.

g. The feeling of *enlarged participation,* other things being equal (pp. 147–148), applies likewise to customer relationships, though I think less easy to identify in the case of customers than in that of employees. Note the appeal of supporting community enterprises and home products and ask if it is not often important to many customers. Observe how important it is in arguments about tariff "policy."

h. The *"condition of communion"* is one of the most important incentives in customer relationships. It is notable in hotels, barrooms, the opera, and country grocery stores. Going where you meet your friends and "your kind of people" and promoting that kind of service has been basic in some businesses and a substantial factor in many.

Maintenance of Schemes of Deterrents

The maintenance of schemes of deterrents to customers is important in many businesses. "Discouraging that kind of trade" is one expression of it. It is accomplished sometimes by price practice, sometimes by insufficient stocks of certain kinds of goods, sometimes by putting stock in inconvenient locations, sometimes by inattention, discrimination, insufficient courtesy, and even discourteous treatment. One can hardly take into account many of the nuances of business practice without recognizing this.

Supervision and Control of Customers

Customers have to be supervised and controlled just as much as employees. The techniques are different. The most notable instance is retail credit practice. Another is professional surveillance; another is analysis of accounts and rejection of those not desirable — in banks, for example.

Inspection of Customers

In many businesses one of the important major functions is the inspection of the behavior of customers in many senses, with a view to rejection of those undesirable, and also to facilitate proper utilization of the advantages the customer receives. Expert inspection of the use the customer makes of his purchase is an important function in telephone, gas, and electric companies and with purveyors of technical equipment and of specialty materials — fertilizers, for example.

Education and Training of Customers

The improper use of goods and services sold is of serious concern in innumerable businesses. Hence much advertising, a great part of sales effort, much technical investigation, even schools and lectures for customers, and expensive pamphlets and books of instruction, are commonplace. Not only is this educational work necessary to specific use of merchandise and services, but also much of it, just as in the case of employees, is necessary to secure an indispensable cooperative state of mind. In the case of which I am best advised — telephone service — not only incorrect practice but non-cooperative attitudes can disturb the functioning of the technical system as a whole. The "morale" of customers in many businesses is of vital importance, not from the political point of view, but from the technical point of view, a fact that seems to be missed in many discussions of advertising and of public relations work. A dissatisfied customer is likely to misuse what he buys from sheer resentment.

Brief as this discussion is, I believe it will be sufficient to show that my statement of the function of "securing the personal services that constitute the material of organization" requires little, if any, "translation" to apply to customers, and that the "puzzle" is solved by reference to obvious, or at least common, facts of everyday observation.

Note that we are not here dealing in analogies. I do not say that the treatment of customers is analogous to that of employees. I say that the nature of the cooperative acts is the same in both cases under the definition of organization I am using; and that the nature of the behavior required to elicit such acts is the same, as shown by experience. I have long believed this. The "horse sense" way of saying it is that human nature is human nature whether you call it "employee" or "customer." But this is no more than a "wise crack," perhaps without much sense until it can be shown to stand up to analysis. It is a very great gain in intellectual control when it can be established that things regarded as different are similar, and that the processes of dealing with them often regarded as different are likewise similar. Here it is accomplished by the concept of organization as I have defined it, and this concept is grounded in recognized facts.

I have not extended the argument to wholesalers, investors of various kinds, distributors, to whom it equally applies, because the reader can readily do this for himself, if sufficiently acquainted with business to find the above analysis intelligible. The greatest mental difficulty is that we are habituated, in economics and in business ideologies, to make the inducements the primary concern, whereas in the more fundamental study of cooperation it is the process of coordination of acts which is primary, inducements being conditions and the personal objectives of cooperation.

Let me repeat. The confusion on this matter generally will arise from the fact that we are "economically" minded, not "organizationally" minded. Our views of what occurs in business behavior are unfortunately too often in ideas of economic, not sociological, theories. The emphasis in economics (and in the commercial aspects of business) is upon the things exchanged, the tangible inducements to action, the ratios between inducements — i.e., prices — not upon the acts of cooperation as such. The distinction is of first importance. It was inadequately discussed in chapter xvi. We shall not well understand what we are doing if we confine our theory of business behavior to economics, though we also shall not understand it sufficiently if we leave the economic aspects out of account.

II. Conceptual Equipment for the Analysis of Organization and Management

The concept of organization set forth above undoubtedly at first sight seems artificial and unrealistic to many. For most routine everyday purposes I would agree that this is so. But it may well be not so, if the purpose is to establish a means of investigation and communication of a scientific character. In advocating the concept of organization I have used from this point of view, I shall discuss the subject under two heads as follows: (i) The Appropriate Level of Discourse; and (ii) The Conceptual Equipment for an Adequate Theory of Organization Management.

i. the appropriate level of discourse

A desirable qualification for many executive positions is the capacity of discussing the same subject in several "languages," depending upon the audience and also the purpose. I shall call such languages "levels of discourse." These are not quite the same as "levels of abstraction," since in many kinds of discourse gestures, facial expressions, type of examples and illustrations, and the extent of emotional behavior are as important as words.

The "lowest" level is that of physical demonstration — pointing out what to see, pointing to conditions, results. Discourse at this level is the nearest to "reality" and the concrete. There is no approximately adequate substitute for it in learning how to do things and in acquiring a certain experimental knowledge. It is basic, as can be seen from the development and training of children. But in itself it has narrow limitations for the acquiring of understanding or for securing knowledge applicable to the control and direction of the things to be done.

At the other extreme is the level of scientific discourse which ultimately is concerned with the broadest generalizations rigorously defined, logically consistent and non-contradictory, and often highly abstract. It too has narrow limitations. It teaches the individual little about how to do things; it is incomplete and insufficient for concrete behavior; but it greatly widens the understanding, expands the possibilities of control, and corrects illusions, hence it permits the avoidance of errors from illusions, in practical operations. What is equally important, it furnishes suitable concepts and terms and ways of looking at things, for use on a lower level of discourse, thereby promoting much wider analysis of practical experience and greater collaboration among competent men than would otherwise be possible. I need only refer to engineering and the practice of medicine to illustrate. Both involve experience and talents that are in no sense scientific, but neither could be very effective if underlying the practice there were no sciences, and no acquirement of scientific methods of work, and no comprehensive "sound" theories.

Between these two extremes are the various levels of practical discourse. They are nearly all highly abstract but they differ in generality. Leading executives (business or others) in their discourse amongst themselves approach, though not very closely, the scientific (usually without knowing it), and their conversation is full of assumptions and fictions which correspond to fundamental concepts and hypotheses of science. They, of course, rely upon concrete experience and dip down into the detail of "what's going on," as the scientist goes back to experiment and controlled observation and analysis.

In the absence of science, discourse at these intermediate levels is often rather incoherent and awkward, except among those who work closely together in restricted situations. Hence the comparison of experience and the observation of the significant are difficult, and the enunciation of non-sense profuse. On the basis of attendance as a member at probably not less than 2,000 meetings of boards and committees of business institutions and associations, I should say that very frequently a few well-directed questions as to meaning of words would disrupt the apparent agreement. "To ask what it means" is a favorite bit of disruptive tactics in some kinds of political work.

Most people, of course, prefer a level of discourse considerably below the scientific unless they are scientists. So do I prefer non-scientific discourse in its place — where I am most of the time. As a matter of everyday practice I use several levels of discourse about the same subject for different situations. I should no more think of using the language of my book in most of the practical work I do than I would ordinarily of talking electronic physics to a telephone repairman, though he is working all the time with electrical circuits and apparatus, and has to know a good deal about them. Nevertheless, I think electronic physics an exceedingly practical and realistic as well as a scientific subject.

These remarks are pertinent because of the tendency of some

readers to disparage the attempt at a scientific approach because it may not be of immediate practical use. I should indeed insist that it is not of immediate practical use; but this does not mean that there is no utility, other than the satisfaction of curiosity as to the sociology and psychology of organization, in the approach used. I believe, on the contrary, that it is of practical importance, in view of the great problems of large-scale operations in business, government, and education, that many contribute what they can to the laborious process of attaining sound generalizations about social cooperation. We still need to achieve an adequate theoretical basis for training in the administrative professions. It will be laborious to attain and laborious to master, as in any other science, and this without reference to the merits of any particular exposition.

II. THE CONCEPTUAL EQUIPMENT FOR AN ADEQUATE THEORY OF ORGANIZATION MANAGEMENT

The following remarks are written as of possible value to those who give serious thought to general matters of economics, organization, and administration, but who find it difficult to be interested in attempts to establish fundamental theory, with its meticulous definitions, postulates, and elaboration of concepts, hypotheses, and abstractions.

I take it that a theory is a comprehensive explanation of a situation, of a state of affairs, of a course of events or action, of what takes place. Many theories are bad, many are trivial, some are important, some are good, none are final. Those that are bad do not fit the facts, they do not explain. Those that are trivial relate to minor matters of local and personal interest, where their importance is largely that of aiding personal decision. Those that are important cover wider matters of general interest or concern. Those that are good fit the facts in general, are self-consistent, prove useful in discovering new facts of importance, can be widely accepted, and serve to permit communication of facts, knowledge, and ideas with efficiency and precision.

1. Theories are not final because, though they must fit the facts approximately, they serve to change the facts, not only by making it possible to discover new facts which must then be taken into account, but by modifying what we conceive to be a fact. For a fact is not a thing or event, it is a statement about a thing or event, and it is impossible, or nearly so, to make a statement without implying some theory of events — what is "important," for instance. Thus every statement of fact is an abstraction. It refers to some aspect only of events. Take the fact that "John Doe paid Richard Roe ten dollars." This refers to an event (or series of events). It might be possible to write two pages of facts about that event but most of them would be entirely without interest. Yet if you will listen to the court evidence when there is litigation about whether John Doe paid Richard Roe, you will find that some of the uninteresting facts in these supposed two pages suddenly have become very interesting and important. However, no one by the most extended statement conceivably possible for a human being could completely describe this event.

The observed aspects of things or events about which statements of fact are made are called phenomena. Thus a fact is a statement of an idea, something conceived in the mind, about a phenomenon, an observed aspect of a thing or event. Such an idea is also known as a concept. Thus theories are made up of concepts as statements of fact and must fit the concepts that are "current," "accepted," or "established," depending upon the level of discourse. Ordinarily, however, we do not use the word "concept" to cover a simple idea about a detail or "single" event.

The kind of facts just discussed are "concrete." They concern us in the ordinary routine of life. They are what workmen use, and what clerks handling vouchers are occupied with. Executives have relatively little to do with them, but hate to admit it except when in the mood to say they "can't be bothered with detail."

2. A statement of fact may be not only what we conceive to be a thing or single event, but about a whole collection of events regarded with respect to a particular aspect of them. This general fact is an aggregate of many similar facts. "A million men voted yesterday" is such a fact. This also is a concept but a more "dignified" one than those relating to "simple" facts. Poincaré said that all generalization is a hypothesis.[3] It can only be stated on the basis of inference from complex evidence largely indirect. No one ever saw a million men vote or even more than a very small fraction of that number voting. What a million men did depends upon what you mean by man (it does not in this case include boy, for example, but may include women), what you mean by voting (are "repeaters" included or excluded?), and many other things, such as "Who said so?" Thus this fact is constructed from ordinary facts observable by individuals, with the aid of an elaborate theory or set of theories. It is a fact secured by evidence, the validity of which is determined by some theory.

These are the facts of a kind which chiefly concerns executives. They often like to believe them concrete, for "facts are facts." The more positively we believe a generalization to be true, the more "real," the more "concrete" the fact seems to be. To the man who won the election of a million votes it is a very concrete event. Still he hopes it will not be necessary "to go behind the returns."

3. There are other ideas or concepts which are not facts in the sense that they can be directly inferred from evidence of observation and theory, but which are products of general knowledge, theories, experience, the sense of things, imagina-

[3] H. Poincaré, "Science and Hypothesis" in *The Foundations of Science* (New York, The Science Press, 1929), p. 133.

tion. They are constructed out of whole cloth, as it were, though not arbitrarily and with no reference to experience, to help give an explanation, that is, to help make a theory. They are likely to be deemed good if the theory works, that is, if the theory explains particular and general facts satisfactorily. The question whether such concepts are true or false often makes no sense, and as to some of the most useful it can be asserted that they never can be proven true or false.[4] Their function is to organize ideas and facts. This is the kind of thing I mean by "concept" or "construct" in *The Functions*.

The use of such concepts or leading ideas is to furnish the framework of a theory, that is, a workable explanation of a vast number of facts. It is necessary to have such a framework to get "basing points," as it were, some place to start getting order out of bewildering chaos and to have enough rigidity — "consistency" — to keep things in order long enough at least to consider them. It is necessary to have more than one such concept to make a theory. If the reader will regard a fundamental concept as merely an important way of looking at things, he will understand that a complex set of facts requires more than one way of looking at things — different angles of view, more than one dimension. I call a set of fundamental concepts furnishing the framework of a theory a "conceptual scheme." It is not complete. Like most such things, this conceptual scheme will have to evolve in the process of using what we have.

Fundamental concepts may be regarded as of two kinds: those which are structural, and those which are dynamic. The first relates to general aspects of the subject that are relatively stable, fixed. The dynamic kind relates to the general ideas as to "how it works," of movement or change. The distinction is more or less arbitrary but convenient. Thus in the theory

[4] H. Poincaré, *passim*.

of the human body structural concepts make up the science of anatomy, and dynamic concepts relate to physiology, notwithstanding that the structural parts of the body are always changing, and much of the physiology may be regarded as comparatively stable — circulation of the blood, for example. In social matters I look upon the structural concepts as stable in the sense that a whirlpool is stable. They are statements of stable relationships between incessantly successive series of acts giving a sense, a feeling, of something fixed.

The conceptual scheme of the theory of formal organization on which *The Functions of the Executive* was constructed follows:

Principal Structural Concepts

1. *The Individual.* Chapter ii, and incidentally throughout. As a preparation for important work with human beings as salesman, politician, teacher, personnel man, or executive this concept is important; for I believe all men tend to regard others in two extremes: (1) either as they would like to regard themselves — completely exercising free will, and independent; or (2) as completely nonindividual, "dumb," responsive nonentities. Appropriate personal behavior is acquired by intuition, social experience, hard knocks; but beyond the range of strictly personal behavior some kind of intellectual comprehension seems advisable if not necessary. But the doctrine is difficult, labored, abstract, abstruse.

2. *The Cooperative System.* Chiefly chapter v.

3. *The Formal Organization.* Chapters vi and vii. They have an important defect in not containing the discussion of the relationship of customers to organization.

4. *The Complex Formal Organization.* Chapters viii, x, and xv, and pp. 175–181.

5. *The Informal Organization.* Chapter ix and pp. 223–226.

Principal Dynamic Concepts

1. *Free Will.* Chapters ii, xi, 1st half chapter xii, much of chapters xvi and xvii.
2. *Cooperation.* Chapters iii, iv, v, xvi. Defective in the omission of cases of simple economic exchange as a type of cooperation.
3. *Communication.* Chapters vii, viii, xii, xv.
4. *Authority.* Chapter xii.
5. *The Decisive Process.* Chapters xii, xiii, xiv. It is called in the book "The Theory of Opportunism." So far as I know, this concept, like that of the formal organization, may be original. I believe it to be for sociological purposes by far the most important suggestion. It is not sufficiently developed in the book to make this apparent, and would probably need a book to make it so. The requirements of decisive behavior (as contrasted with responsive behavior) are such as to be a chief determinant of ideas, norms, conventions, institutions, and social habits (including business routines and devices), and of organization itself as necessary equipment for the exercise of the propensity to make conscious decisions.
6. *Dynamic Equilibrium.* Chapter xi and especially chapter xvi. This concept I believe is very close to that which Professor Copeland called "adaptation to changing conditions."
7. (Executive) *Responsibility.* Chapter xvii.

Roughly, Parts I and II are the "anatomy" or structure of cooperation; Parts III and IV are its physiology or economy.

VI

ON PLANNING FOR WORLD GOVERNMENT[1]

If we could first know where we are and whither we are tending, we could better judge what to do and how to do it. — ABRAHAM LINCOLN

It is the greatest of mistakes to believe that it has required the high-grade intelligence of mankind to construct an elaborate social organization. A particular instance of this error is the prevalent assumption that any social routine whose purposes are not obvious to our analysis is thereby to be condemned as foolish. — ALFRED NORTH WHITEHEAD

And if the world is to come before you for judgment, are you unfit to decide the most trivial cases? — SAINT PAUL

MY purpose is to discuss limitations of social and political planning. They should be emphasized, I think, to avoid erroneous effort, false hopes, and disillusionment in connection with the plans for world government now being developed and exploited. First, I should like to present considerations which lead me to believe this purpose worthy of the attention of the readers. Then I shall offer some general observations on various kinds of planning and their effects. Third, I shall present a few historical illustrations of failures of planning. Next, and mainly, I shall discuss structural aspects of organization in order to suggest kinds of organization problems and the kinds of means and obstacles that need to be taken into account in political and social planning. Finally, following a short summary, I shall give brief suggestions on the theory of planning.

[1] Reprinted from *Approaches to World Peace,* a symposium edited by Lyman Bryson, Louis Finkelstein and Robert M. MacIver, copyright 1944 by the Conference on Science, Philosophy and Religion in Their Relation to the Democratic Way of Life, Inc. Prepared for the conference of the above name held at the Faculty Club, Columbia University, September, 1943.

I

To maintain world peace, it is now generally supposed, calls for some system of improved world government or organization. Such a system, like governments in the past, could come about through blind evolution. However, many men have aspired to make sure of good social organization by design. They have recently been impressed, perhaps, with the extent and success of planning on the small scale, or have been intrigued with planning on the large scale as attributed to the totalitarian governments, or they have accepted socialist or communist doctrines in which the feasibility of successful large-scale planning is a basic assumption; and so they have hoped that more perfect systems of government could be attained by deliberate planning.

No doubt, a great number of schemes for world organization could be constructed. They might differ widely in the degree of reliance upon formal organization; in emphasis upon political, economic, social, or religious forces and conditions; in extent of dependence upon authoritarian methods as contrasted with those of free agreement; in the scope of the matters reserved for centralized control; in the degree to which they are provisional "realistic" schemes or ultimate ideal plans; and in other respects. But they would all have this in common: they would appear to be quite simple, compared with the immense intricacies of world-wide social life.

The complex relationships involved in plans for large-scale organization and the wide knowledge required to discuss them cogently make it probable that the leaders in such planning will be chiefly intellectuals, students, and observers who have not had much responsible experience in guiding organizations. Accordingly, we might expect that much of the presentation and discussion of such plans will be in terms of broad generalizations, high abstractions, and dogmatic assumptions.

These tendencies will be strengthened by the emotional appeal of the high ideals of the world order and world peace. Indeed, the very complexities will lead to such dangerous characteristics if discussion and writing are to be kept within workable limits. We may also expect the political advocates and often the opponents of any such plans to give emphasis to what is known or thought to be known, to grant little attention to factors concerning which there is recognized ignorance, and scarcely even to admit the probability of crucial areas of ignorance not recognized.

Surely there is in all this the possibility that our planning for world organization may lead or add to bitterness and strife, division, and disillusionment. Moreover, there is danger that failure of plans or refusal to accept particular plans will be ascribed to "politics," selfishness, and hypocrisy. Of these, no doubt, there will always be a plenitude; but if there is failure or apparent obstinacy, it may better be first assumed that there are more fundamental causes which name-calling tends to obscure, and of which, perhaps, the planners were unaware.

II

To attain better perspective regarding wide-scale, long-run planning, it may be helpful to record a few general remarks about planning itself. At this place I shall present them in terms of an everyday approach. At the conclusion of this paper I shall offer further remarks in terms of a more thorough analysis.

Probably the chief analogy in the minds of most political planners is the planning of concrete structures made by engineers or architects and the designing of particular mechanical devices. Undoubtedly this type of planning is the simplest and the most successful of all. Yet, even in such planning errors are numerous, though seldom of public knowledge or interest. Two kinds of errors may be noted: that in which failure is unequivocal, and that which eventuates into structures or devices quite different from, but as or more useful than, those contemplated. The latter are seldom acknowledged as failures and are often counted successes even by those with intimate knowledge of facts. In witness of this, the following account may be of interest. In the early nineteen-twenties, I had the privilege of aiding the late J. J. Carty, then vice-president and chief engineer of the American Telephone and Telegraph Company, prepare an address for the inaugural meeting of the New York Regional Plan, under the auspices of the Russell Sage Foundation. General Carty said to me in the course of that work: "You know, we often make plans which eventuate into achievements quite different from, and much better than, those we contemplated. Then we are apt to credit ourselves in all seriousness and sincerity with accomplishments that are really fortuitous. We put in our thumbs and pull out the plums and cry: 'What great engineers are we!'"

I shall not stop to show how evolutionary in fact is the process of designing concrete physical structures and devices. But I would point out that the real planning associated with such structures is much broader and more comprehensive than the bare designing of the physical elements, which are indispensable but subsidiary. For example, very few buildings are designed to be mere physical structures. Of course, they are intended to be useful in particular ways, to be of value to certain kinds of clients, to have uses of certain minimum values, and to involve outlays of certain maximums. Judged by even this curtailed list of limiting considerations of the planned project, failures are numerous. The completed building, if successfully designed as a structure, may be but a part of an unsuccessfully planned undertaking. It has perhaps cost more than intended, or its uses are worth less than expected, or the kind of uses is different than contemplated. To few are these errors evident or known. The permanent structure stands for all to see — the apparent evidence of successful planning, though in fact it frequently was a failure from the decisive position of the planner.

However, I think it may be granted without much reservation that planning with respect to specific structures and devices may on the whole be accepted as in general successful and indispensable to intelligent behavior in even simple affairs or to complex technological systems. This is nearly equivalent to saying that planning, with respect to a single strategic factor,[2] in a total situation *assumed* to be fixed in all, or nearly all, other respects, is in general successful and often indispensable. It involves, however, the "all other things being equal" fallacy common to all planning. Whether this logically fallacious assumption is practically valid can usually be learned only from trial and error.[3]

When we turn from planning with respect to strategic *factors* to the planning of new complex *systems* comprised of numerous independent and dependent variables, there seems to me to be no evidence it has ever been more than fortuitously successful on a large scale. Social and political planning is

[2] For explanation of "strategic factor" and of the nature of thinking required to determine purposeful action, I must refer the reader to chapter xiv, "The Theory of Opportunism," in my *The Functions of the Executive,* Harvard University Press, 1938. See also Karl Mannheim, *Man and Society in an Age of Reconstruction,* Harcourt, Brace and Co., 1940, *passim,* especially pp. 147–155.

[3] Good businessmen, competent executives, wise politicians, and capable scientists in my observation all evince great caution, in their respective fields, regarding the probable effect of even small changes in a complex system in the absence of specifically successful experience or experiment. They are sceptical of the very common arguments in the form "Since all else is equal, this change will effect this and only this particular result." This kind of confidence is of great influence in the field of the present essay, so that it may be useful to publish a letter written to demonstrate in simple mathematics the nature of the fallacy by the late Professor Lawrence J. Henderson. This will be found in the appendix to this paper.

necessarily of this kind. The best simple illustration of this known to me is furnished by an example of Pareto, a leading mathematical economist of the past century. Taking a supposititious community of 100 individuals, having for exchange only 700 products, even under absurdly oversimplified assumptions he calculated that 70,699 simultaneous equations were required to determine the prices equalizing demand and supply. He noted that for a society of 40,000,000 people and several thousand products, the number of equations would be fabulous. This led him to remark that the simplest practicable solution was the market, not the mathematician.[4] This example seems most apt to the present subject, since I would regard an economic system, or rather the economic aspects of a social system, as much simpler than a political or social system as a whole.

III

The practical significance of the preceding general observations is at least suggested by the study of history.

In trying to build social and political systems in the past, men seldom knew what they were doing, though some thought they did; and so frequently what came about was not what they intended. In support of this I have sometimes recalled the conquest of Greece and Macedonia by the Roman Republic against its own wishes and policy, the British political control of India which both the East India Company and the British Government sought to avoid for many years, and the change of position in the Reformation from one directed toward reform of administrative, fiscal, and political conditions in the

---

[4] Vilfredo Pareto, *Manuel d'Economie Politique,* Deuxième Edition, Marcel Giard, Paris, 1927, pp. 233, 234. *"Dans ce cas (i.e.,* a large economy) *les rôles seraient changées et ce ne seraient plus les mathématiques qui viendraient en aide à l'économie politique, mais l'économie politique qui viendrait en aide aux mathématiques."*

Church to that of a conflict of dogma. But in connection with political and social planning, the following two modern examples are especially apposite:

A. Lawrence Lowell, asked to illustrate from history the principles brought out in a symposium at the Harvard Tercentenary, said that his utmost was to take some specific method of attaining a political result and describe a particular case of its use. Taking the British Parliamentary System, he showed that it was by no means contemplated by the men who brought it about. In a fundamental respect, its lack of separation of legislative and executive powers, the reverse of the original intention expressed in the Act of Settlement of 1702, was actually put into effect. Indeed, this occurred almost immediately after the adoption of the Act which forbade any one holding an office of place or profit under the crown from having a seat in the House of Commons. Yet three distinguished writers — Montesquieu, the Swiss DeLolme, and, most notably, Sir William Blackstone — all wrote of English Government as if literally in accordance with a statute which was not of effect in the respect stated above, and of a philosophy of government definitely contradicted by concrete practice known to them. Moreover, the books of these men in their day were accepted by the British as correctly presenting the theory and practice of their Government.[5] It appears to be the wish and a common practice of men, if the circumstances permit of it, to assert that they are doing what, and only what, they *say* they are doing, or to say and believe that they have done what they intended to do.

Again: The framers of the American Constitution provided that the president and the vice-president should be chosen by an electoral college, not by popular election. Though the Constitution remained unchanged, the intention was early frus-

[5] Abbott Lawrence Lowell, "An Example from History" in *Factors Determining Human Behavior*, Harvard University Press, 1937.

trated by the pledging of candidates for the electoral college to nominees for these offices. This was inherent in the national party system of politics. Not only was the national party system not provided for in the Constitution — it still is not — but it was deemed undesirable. This most important part of the "unwritten" constitution of American government developed contrary to plan. It may be argued that the party system is something external and auxiliary to the government proper, yet in fact it affected almost every aspect of government so that little of it works as originally intended or imagined. For example: the organization of legislative work is quite different from what it could be under a nonparty system. So also are the obligations, degrees of independence, and the loyalties of the principal executive officers. The criterion for the selection of the personnel of courts and of administrative and semijudicial boards is bipartisan rather than nonpartisan, as it would be under a nonparty system. It seems to me probable, also, that the organization of parties of country-wide scope made the relationships of the states to the federal government very different from what they otherwise would have been.

Facts and cases of the same import as these few could be multiplied indefinitely. At first consideration they seem to justify Brooks Adams's statement: "Another conviction forced upon my mind, by the examination of long periods of history, was the exceedingly small part played by conscious thought in moulding the fate of men." [6] The error of Adams's conclusion, I think, lies in underestimating the effect of deliberate thought because it has not been a single determinant nor a dominant factor of the course of events. This arises, I judge, from the belief that effective thinking for social control is analogous to planning of a mere physical structure. At root it comes from failure to note the difference of function of thought when di-

[6] *The Law of Civilization and Decay*, Alfred H. Knopf & Co., New York, 1943, p. 58.

rected to human action in a concrete changing environment, strategic thinking, and thought directed to abstract propositions in a fixed isolated system. Lowell understood this, and so did not deny the role of "conscious thought in moulding the fate of men" nor, on the other hand, overestimate its possibilities as implicitly as most planners seem to me to do. Hence, he could write:

The object of this paper is . . . merely to point out that men, like animals, may attain a self-consistent and harmonious system of conducting their affairs *by a process of striving for immediate intentional objects,* if the conditions happen to be such as to lead to a system of that kind; and this although the actors themselves do not contemplate it, or even if the result is quite contrary to their preconceived ideas.[7] [Italics mine]

IV

These examples from history can properly be only suggestive of the need of circumspection on the part of planners and of caution on the part of their followers. It could be argued, moreover, that modern science and technologies have made a new world, requiring and permitting a new kind of management.[8] More to the point, then, and also more constructive as presenting materials for the real solution of real problems, would be the study of existing organizations and of successful and unsuccessful experience with them. However, with respect to our capacity for large-scale social planning, it is unfortunate but significant that little is as yet known with assurance concerning organizations and their operation. But that little is clearly pertinent to the present subject. I propose to present that which appeals to me as most important under the following headings: (1) Informal Organization; (11) Lateral and Scalar Organization; and (111) Two Problems of Structural Balance in Scalar Organization. A few introductory remarks

[7] Lowell, *op. cit.,* p. 132.
[8] This is, indeed, the position of Mannheim, *op. cit.*

will make the meaning of these headings more intelligible.

The exposition which follows will be fragmentary and cannot be comprehensive. It is intended only to be suggestive and illustrative of the kind of problems to be faced by organization planners. Accordingly, I shall limit it to some major matters of organization structure, because that is the least difficult aspect of organization. Thus, I shall mention only incidentally, if at all, the more delicate and intricate problems of the dynamics of organization — such as their modes of operation; the relations of individuals to them; the functions of leadership; the effect of organization upon individuals; incentives; the fictions inherently necessary; the nature and apparatus of authority; the judicial functions; the numerous and complex kinds of balances required. I intend, as it were, to limit myself to certain problems of the anatomy of organization and to disregard its physiology.

From the standpoint of structure all organizations reveal three kinds of material. To the first and most fundamental, I have given the name "informal organization." It pervades a society or any subdivision of it. It provides the bases for, and is itself structured by, formal organizations. These are of two kinds. I shall focus what I have to say about the two kinds of formal organization on the contrasts between them; for the choice between them is the primary problem of world formal organization.

Finally, assuming that rightly or wrongly an effective decision were made to organize the world hierarchically, as many advocate, I shall discuss merely two structural problems of the scalar type of organization which seem to me to be of first importance to the planners of such an organization.

I. INFORMAL ORGANIZATION

The words "society," "community," and "informal organization," for very general purposes are nearly synonymous.

"Society" perhaps puts the emphasis upon a "group of people" who somehow have a distinguishable existence as a group living in some sense in common. "Community" puts the emphasis not upon the group but upon the living in common and upon interdependence through communication. It expresses the generality of relationships among the people of a group which makes of it a society. "Informal organization" puts the emphasis upon the interdependence of the concrete behavior of those comprised in the social group. It refers to regularity in the functional aspect of a society. A group is a society because it is made into a community by informal organization. A society *is* because of informal organization and its consequences — community, man-made works, culture, formal organization; and each society may be said to *have* an informal organization.

Informal organization develops presumably out of propinquity between parents and between them and their children, between their children, between those entering into cooperative relationships by reason of geographical propinquity, and then between those who have the figurative propinquity of common intellectual and moral or spiritual understanding.

The interactions between the members of a society in the aggregate constitute informal organization. These interactions consist chiefly of physical contact and acts of physical cooperation and communication, partly by relatively crude means but principally by the use of language, especially oral language. This interaction occurs as an observed fact in repetitive habitual ways and patterns involving the development and use of common symbols and of a stock of conceptions about the things symbolized. All of this results not only in habitual ways of doing things and in habitual ways of communication but also in attitudes, habitual ways of looking at things, fixed stocks of conceptions about things, and habitual reactions to events and communication. The precise nature of the interactions is rarely discernible by direct observation, and only an extremely small part of the aggregate of interactions is even available at all to the observation of "outsiders." To observe is extremely difficult because the intent of, and the attitude connected with, overt acts, and the extent to which physical action is itself an unconscious means of communications, and the unexpressed or inexpressible reactions to acts, are essential parts of human interaction but are intangible and imponderable. Hence, we know of informal organization by our personal experience and perhaps chiefly through its more important distinguishable effects. These are mores, customs, commonly held aversions, persistent beliefs, conventions, codes of morals, institutions, language, and certain concrete evidences such as arts and architecture, folksongs and folklore, literature, rites and ceremonies, and *formal organizations*. These discernible objective effects of, or arising from, informal organization are, I think, what is usually meant by "culture."

Some of the concrete action in informal organization is responsive, without definite purpose, unintentional, imitative. Some is volitional, purposeful, intended. It all contributes to, and is a part of, the ordering and unity of the whole; but it is characteristic of informal organization that none of the *organizational* (or social) effect of its concrete activities is willed or intended. Informal organization as organization is unconscious. As is similarly true of most of the physiological processes of the living body, it is nonetheless real for that.

Informal organization dominates and establishes limits to the personal and social behavior of the members of a society. This may be accounted for by several reasons. Two of them are: First, the complexities of the interactions between the members of a society are so great that they must largely be kept orderly by habit. The important relationships must be usually stereotyped. Second, the possibility of communication and of having overt behavior understood depends upon conformance to habitual patterns and to commonly accepted norms and upon adaptation to the currently held conceptions. We may say that these reasons underlie the strong resistance of societies to radical alterations of their informal organizations by external pressures. They would destroy the capacity for effective behavior and the unity that depends upon unpremeditated immediate responsive communication. The importance of this is quite easily seen from the reactions of high professional groups against arbitrary changes in specialized languages or against alterations of the customary practices of professional behavior. No fact seems to me to be of more importance to be taken into account by social and political planners. What alterations of informal organization either can or will be accepted by a society is at once the most recalcitrant and the most speculative of practical problems.[9] It is, in my view, the most fundamental problem in planning comprehensive formal organization, since the area it can cover is more or less limited to that in which there is the primary unity of an informal organization.

The effect of ever-widening contact between peoples is to expand informal organization. This is a striking characteristic of the modern world which now constitutes in a qualified sense a single society. This trend is restrained, however, by barriers and is opposed and modified by political forces, i.e., by the segmentation of informal organization through the divi-

[9] This highly condensed treatment of the subject is, I hope, sufficient for present purposes. It is covered more fully in my book, op. cit., in chapter ix, "Informal Organizations and Their Relation to Formal Organizations." The conceptions there set forth were so far as I am aware chiefly based on experience and observation in operating in organizations, rather than on the literature. Since writing the book, I have studied two important books which, in general, confirm my views. I would refer the reader to them. The first is Ferdinand Toennies, Gemeinschaft und Gesellschaft, now available in English as Fundamental Concepts of Sociology by Toennies and Loomis, translator and supplementer, American Book Co., 1940. The second is Community, by R. M. MacIver, 3rd edition, reprint of 1936, The Macmillan Co.

sive effects of formal organizations and of the functional specializations accompanying them.

The barriers to the world-wide extension of informal organizations are primarily geographical, limiting physical travel and commerce. Today at least equally important may be the barriers of diverse languages, customs, religious beliefs, and cultures, usually, perhaps too exclusively, ascribed to geographical circumstances.

For formal organizations tend also to create such barriers. Each formal organization is the expression of explicit cooperative purposes and when once established each tends to create a sub-society of its own. The reason for this is that the needs of communication in a formal organization transcend the capacities of formal channels or facilities. A condition of formal unity depends upon the establishment and maintenance of informal unity and a capacity of habitual behavior and mutual understanding which permits of correct responsive action in a myriad of ways. Thus the function of informal organization in formal organizations is both communication and the stabilizing of behavior.

Segmentation of informal organization by formal organization structure may be restricting the spread of informal organization more rapidly than improved communications are expanding it. Whereas formerly a single society, say English society, was subdivided into local societies geographically limited, with divergencies of dialect and local custom, now the subdivisions arise more out of attachment to specific formal organizations — a government department, a business organization, or a professional body. In these a large part of the activities of individuals occurs. They are the foci of much of their major interests. The specializations usually involve highly special jargons and often special formal languages. Thus, increasingly those who speak only English speak in specialized English sub-languages not generally comprehensible; and the attitudes and conditioning of such groups vary widely. The unity of the informal organization of our society tends to break down through the development of innumerable secondary informal organizations with customs and languages of their own. The very technologies and the formal organizations necessary to their development and use tend to divide and break down informal organization while providing the very means for its extension.

Nevertheless, a widespread and large society seems impossible without an elaborate network of formal organizations tending to the condition just described. In my opinion, this does not imply, as some suppose, the inevitable breakdown of our civilization. It suggests only that an equilibrium between opposing tendencies must be established if breakdown is to be avoided. Conceivably there are several, if not many, combinations of elements, forces, and structures in which such equilibria could obtain, and an infinite number in which equilibrium is impossible. With changes in size, structure, and functions, the attainment or maintenance of the necessary equilibrium is a matter of progressive organic readjustment. For this reason, the conception of static design implicit in most planning does not seem appropriate to general social organization.

What has been said of informal organization here is intended primarily to make intelligible the observations to follow on formal organization. However, informal organization is so fundamental to all social organization, its power is so great, its inertia and resistance to deliberate change so manifest, and the problem of inducing in it changes desired, and only those desired, is so delicate and complex that its bearing on social and political planning will surely not be missed. The greatest difficulty confronting the social and political planner is the intangible, imponderable, vague forces and inertias of informal organization. For dealing with them, there is available a certain amount of political and propaganda technique. This is itself a product of trial and error and of the prepossessions and predilections of a popular psychology, reflecting the very thing it purports to work upon, so there is little of this technique on which the planner may solidly base his fundamental plans.

II. LATERAL AND SCALAR ORGANIZATION CONTRASTED

The difficulty the planner faces with respect to formal organization is only somewhat less formidable. For the actual operation of such organizations there is a great body of technical apparatus — contract law, the law of partnerships and corporations, the constitutions and statutes concerning governmental organization, and the limitless mass of rules, regulations, routines, practices — the internal law of each organization.[10] These are almost altogether concerned with practical operating systems and do not by themselves furnish an apparatus for the comprehension of organizations, such as is required for fundamental planning of vast organizations in a new world.

However, because the planning of organization so largely refers in general to its formal aspects, it is desirable for the purposes of this paper to deal with certain problems of this subject. In doing so it will be convenient to employ a few technical terms and conceptions — crude, not of general acceptance, almost constructed *ad hoc*. If this tries the reader's patience, it will illustrate an important point — world planners are necessarily attempting to plan vast and complex structures with primitive and defective equipment.

When men are bound through informal organization into a community of interests, understanding, and ideals, the maintenance of the community and their personal interests both lead to the formation of explicit cooperative undertakings to

[10] The extent of private or internal law in formal organizations with respect to the maintenance of discipline alone is quite formidable. See Alfred Legal and Brethe de la Gressaye: *Le Pouvoir Disciplinaire dans les Institutions Privées,* Librairie du Recueil Sirey, Paris, 1938.

accomplish consciously recognized purposes. What those purposes are, what purposes may be excluded, what method of organization will be acceptable, what will be unacceptable, how attractive these organizations may be made to the motives of individuals, the limitations of the methods of operation, the scope and the size of the organizations — all are reflections of the consensus of opinion, and of attitudes, of the people as conditioned by informal organization.

I purpose, in this present section, to define and contrast the two general types of formal [11] organization available. The choice between them is today a most acute problem in economic, social, and political fields whether of world-wide or of narrower scope.

Of the two types of formal organization to be distinguished, the first is that of free agreement — by mutual understanding, by contract, or by treaty. I shall call such organizations "lateral organizations." The second type is "vertical," articulated, hierarchical, scalar. For this type I shall usually use the word "scalar." [12]

A system of cooperative efforts established and maintained by written or oral contract or by treaty is an organization in which the duty of command and the desire to obey are essentially absent. It is nonauthoritarian organization. The primary integration of such an organization is horizontal or lateral. The emphasis is upon the coming into cooperation of

[11] "Formal" in this context is used simultaneously in the figurative sense of "having form" and also in the sense of "explicitly recognized, established, and maintained of public knowledge, its relationships established by statute, written agreement, order, organization chart, or tables of organization."

[12] "Scalar" is the term adopted by James P. Mooney and Alan C. Reiley in *Onward Industry,* Harper & Brothers, New York, 1931, who define it as follows: "A scale means a series of steps; hence, something graduated. In organization, it means the graduation of duties, not according to differentiated functions, for this involves another and distinct principle of organization, but simply according to degrees of authority and corresponding responsibility" (p. 31).

individuals or bodies who are "side by side." The customary legal phraseology "bilateral," "multilateral," etc., reflects this conception. Perhaps the simplest case of lateral organization is that of barter exchange, a short-lived organization. Lateral organizations are usually established for short periods and limited to specific purposes. These purposes are personal to the parties to the agreement and are not inherent in the organization created by agreement. The agreement does not become an end in itself. It does not maintain itself but is maintained by the parties to it severally. Since organization by agreement may be established between despotic states, it is entirely possible that the complexion of a society might be quite authoritarian as a whole, though its widest organization or its organization at the highest level would be formal but lateral, nonauthoritarian; and *vice versa,* an authoritarian government conceivably may permit wide latitude for subordinate organization by free agreement — an authorized *laissez-faire* complex.

Broadly, the political organization of the world between 1905 and 1914 was one of free agreement. Also the economic organization of the world, as well as that within most nations, was one of free agreement. Although this is frequently recognized and stated, it is notable that when we are thinking about organization we are apt unconsciously to overlook the general organization secured by the aggregate of lateral organizations and to think only of scalar organizations.

Turning now to scalar organizations, they are fundamentally authoritarian. In most of them (except states) individuals, it is true, come into them by agreement, but the relationship between subordinate parts and between individuals when operating in them are controlled not by "considerations" fixed as in contracts but by prescriptions to be changed as circumstances may require "for the good of the organization." The primary integration of scalar organization is vertical. Every part except the highest is definitely dependent upon a "higher" part; and every part except the lowest rests upon a foundation of lower parts. Formal relations between parts on the same level, *i.e.,* lateral coordination, are in principle determined by command or instruction, not by agreement. All persons participating are bound together in the accomplishment of common purposes or aims of the organization which are not personal. An injury to one part is regarded as an injury to the whole. A fundamental assumption usually implicit in scalar organizations is their indefinite continuance, even though in fact their mortality is high. Such organizations are so definite that they usually are known by distinctive names, except those of very ephemeral duration.

At least from the point of view of world organization, the most important difference between lateral organization and scalar organization is that the policing and discipline of the former are external to the organization, those of the latter are largely internal. Lateral organizations are "policed" by public opinion, by the "moral community," by custom and habit and social institutions, by the effect of the violation of agreement on the future interest of the violator, for example, *vis-à-vis* future potential agreements. They are also policed within the jurisdiction of states by statutes and by courts and other police authorities. Scalar organization, on the other hand, has to develop and maintain its internal discipline itself, sometimes establishing special police arms to aid in so doing.

It is evident that in so far as world organization could be achieved by deliberate choice of forms of organization, the choice between lateral organization and scalar organization is the primary question. Concerning it there is wide and vehement disagreement. This is evident in the controversies as to whether there should be a superstate of world sovereignty with a world police force, whether there should be organization only by treaty agreement among sovereign states, or whether some intermediate degree of limited articulation and limited world sovereignty — a federal world state — is to be preferred.

Correct selection of these alternatives would require wide knowledge of both past and present conditions and prevision of conditions for a long future. For it is evident that a large-scale organization, advantageous for an immediate short term but the reverse for a long term, would not be knowingly accepted by the planners of world government. This leads to the most difficult speculation of all — the aims of the world society through several generations. For the standard by which a preselected organization is to be chosen must take into account not merely the aims to be served in the present, but those to be served through the successive periods of its life. Now it is clear that in the past the aims and values of succeeding generations have changed considerably. It is to be presumed that they will similarly change in the future. If so, planning and the major choices which must be made in it involve appalling assumptions as to that future. It requires the construction of the "mind" of the future, whereas we admit we are unable to reconstruct the "mind" of the past. For example, Professor H. W. Schneider in *The Puritan Mind* says that the Puritan mind cannot be reconstructed by the twentieth-century scholar, and quotes N. M. Butler: "His was a world into which we cannot enter, even in imagination." [13]

However, let us assume that we can thoroughly comprehend present conditions, are endowed with the gift of prophecy, and can anticipate the aims of values of future generations. Then the choice between lateral organization and scalar organization still presents a formidable problem. On a much smaller scale than the world, it is one which is currently treated in different ways in many different situations. For example, when a business concern ponders whether it should expand its (scalar) organization to produce materials or parts it needs or

[13] Cited and quoted from Jay Wharton Fay, *American Psychology before William James,* Rutgers University Press, 1939, p. 6.

should secure them by contract with other organizations, it is studying whether to expand hierarchically or laterally by free agreement. When several concerns, especially if engaged in complementary rather than competitive enterprises, consider whether they will consolidate or amalgamate into a single concern with several plants (subsidiary organizations) or will remain associated by free contract, they are considering in principle the same problem as that of world government by constitutional and formal organization as against world government by treaty and contract. The solution of the practical problem on the relatively simple and small scale of commercial organization is no doubt nearly always determined by immediate motives and interests, rather than by scientific or reliable practical knowledge of the comparative effectiveness or efficiency of the alternative types of organization, and without concern for the future state of society.

Thus, though there is much experience with the fundamental problem involved in formal world organization, there is little generalized knowledge available from that experience to help the planner. His thought will no doubt be much affected by the many different models of organization of which he knows, but his predilection for or aversion to a particular form of organization will probably be determined by incidental circumstances and by preconceptions.

The practical bearing of this will be clearer if I venture to contrast some of the advantages and disadvantages of lateral and of scalar organization as I understand them.

Lateral organization appears to be generally cheaper in terms of human resources, talents, and leadership abilities, and therefore in terms of overhead costs, than scalar organization, *provided* that freedom and the temporary nature of the specific agreements under the conditions do not lead to an excessive degree of competitiveness and combativeness. The reason for this is that specific decisions are more restricted in scope and relate more to concrete behavior and less to abstract propositions than is the case in scalar organization. In general, men appear able to behave more effectively "in striving for immediate intentional objects" than they do with respect to general objectives of more remote realization. It is noticeable that as scalar organizations become of large size they rapidly outstrip the capacities of all but a very few men to make the major decisions single-handed. Decisions are then in fact largely made by executive organizations, elaborate staff departments, and through a long period of time; *i.e.,* decisions are to a great extent made by reference to an established body of rules and precedents and patterns of action.

This suggests the statement that a general system of organization by free agreement is inherently more flexible and adaptable than that of scalar organizations, though the adaptability of the system as a whole is quite unpremeditated. Indeed, it is the fact that adaptation by scalar organizations must be so much more consciously determined that it makes them less flexible. They are inherently more conservative and less progressive than systems of free agreement, since their leaders have to be concerned simultaneously always with the effect of every decision upon the immediate objective and also with its reaction upon the organization itself. In most scalar organizations it is noticeable that their leaders always, and very often also the rank and file, become concerned with the organization as an end in itself; for the organization is so indispensable a means both to the accomplishment of its purposes and to the satisfaction of the personal motives of the men associated in it, that they conceive only with difficulty that either its true aims or their individual motives and interests can be served without it.

This implies that the number of formal and explicit decisions necessary to be made in scalar organizations is much larger than in a corresponding system of free agreement. This is another element in the greater overhead cost of the former. One indication of this is the greater degree to which differences of opinion and interest must be settled by formal executive and judicial processes in scalar organizations. Corresponding differences for the most part lead to no need for decision in organization by free agreement. *Amour propre* in lateral organizations is purely personal; in scalar organizations, if personal, it becomes organizational also.

A scalar organization has to rely upon the loyalty of those who adhere to it. Upon this the essential authority and discipline depend. The securing and maintenance of this loyalty is a major task at least of its leaders. Since the maintenance of crude loyalty by the progressively advancing satisfaction of self-interest tends to exhaust the resources of an organization and thus to destroy it, the required loyalty must be of the kind which overrides ordinary self-interest, even to the point of submerging or even extinguishing it at times of crisis. When there is failure of the required loyalty, even in a small part, the whole organization is threatened with disintegration.

The need of loyalty is certainly much reduced or is of a different order in organization by free agreement. The loyalty required is to self-interest within a moral code rather than to a specific formal organization, and therefore the discrepancy between a required loyalty to a system and self-interest does not so much arise, or if it does, is personal or local. For this reason, the disruption of the entire system is not so much affected by a breakdown in part of it. For example, if the world were hierarchically organized, a defection by China would tend to disrupt the entire organization, just as the defection of some southern states in 1861 tended to destroy the nation. If the organization were of free agreement, disagreement by China would not necessarily lead to war, or might lead to war of more restricted area.

I have been tempted to say that scalar organization is greatly superior to that of free agreement in respect to coordination and power of accomplishment, but I believe that all that now can be properly said is that for some ends and in some technologies under some conditions it is undoubtedly true that scalar organization is superior to any other and indeed may be the only form of cooperation feasible. This is the case, for example, in the operation of a telephone or railroad system, or of an army or navy. It has not been the case as to the general government of the British Empire, however, which except in the most extreme legalistic sense (dependence upon the British crown) has "progressed" rather from a scalar organization to one of free agreement — from an empire to a commonwealth of nations.

Activities of great complexity seem susceptible of large-size scalar organization only if these activities are capable of being segregated into relatively simple groups in space or in time and if the relation between the segregations is relatively simple, even though the interdependence between them is complete. Whether or not scalar organization can be used will depend to some extent upon the intellectual and technical capacities of leaders or managers to contrive the segregations and workable combinations of them. Moreover, the technique of scalar organization is presumably far from fully developed as yet. Much may also depend upon innovations discoverable by chance.

On the other hand, when there are innumerable interactions not isolatable into small groups having simple interrelations, but on the contrary having a large number of simultaneous interdependencies, scalar organization may be impossible, whereas organization by free agreement has been certainly successful on a wide scale. An excellent illustration is that of market prices and the regulation of supply and of demand for wheat. On a world-wide scale for many years this was accomplished through lateral organization. Contrast this with the difficulties of rationing and price fixing through scalar organizations (price administrations) apparent today. Though many, *e.g.,* communists, believe that scalar organization of society and its economy can succeed, others believe, with Von Mises, that this is impossible in the economic sphere for long periods without the benefit of norms of value established by laterally organized markets external to the hierarchically administered system.[14]

The two types of organization should also be compared with respect to their stability. After much study I cannot find any general conclusion in this matter, except that there seems to be no justification for assuming that lateral organization is less stable than scalar organization. In the field of international government our experience has been chiefly with lateral organization, and we are conscious of its instability and of its wars. But national governments have also been unstable with many rebellions and revolutions. Instability of scalar organization of world-wide scope would spell rebellion. This, if successful, would result in schism and revolution. Technically, these are names for war arising *within* scalar organizations, but in the character of their concrete action, civil wars are not different from other wars.

The final contrast I would draw is between the different tendencies to self-destruction inherent in the two systems of organization. General organization by free agreement secures its flexibility largely by the short-lived aims and the provisional character of its specific lateral organizations. They function in the general setting of competition and under the condition of general freedom. Inherently, such a system lacks its own formal means of preventing friction, strife, and disruptive action. The essential question for this way of organization is

[14] Ludwig von Mises, *Socialism,* The Macmillan Co., New York (undated). See especially pp. 135–142, and the Appendix. However, Schumpeter in his recent *Capitalism, Socialism, and Democracy* (reluctantly) accepts the possibility of scalar (socialist) economic organization.

whether the moral and cultural controls of the disruptive tendencies are sufficient to keep them within bounds so that they do not offset the positive accomplishments of lateral organization.

The essence of scalar organization, on the other hand, is coordination of the whole through centralized authority. Freedom is lessened in order that friction, strife, and disruption may be reduced, security and power thereby being attained and conserved. To this end, a hierarchy is indispensable and also political motives must be superposed upon the economic, social, or religious aims of organization. By "political" I refer to the necessity of elevating the "good of the organization as such" to a superior ranking value though it is a derivative end of cooperation. This political motivation is not confined to the upper ranks of hierarchy, whose status is internal in the organization, but includes the file, which must regard itself, though of inferior rank internally, as superior to corresponding files of other organizations. The presidents and governors are not only of superior rank to the citizen, but the American citizen must be superior, in his own view, to other citizens. The general outranks the colonel, as he the private, but all must evince a devotion implying corresponding general superiority to others.

Both the hierarchical and the political necessities of scalar organizations mean that they are "societies of status" requiring emphasis upon internal security of position. If they move below a certain minimum in this respect, they are affected with lack of stable authority. History and current experience seem to show that this fundamental characteristic of scalar organizations involves a persistent tendency to the exaggeration of the needs of hierarchy and of internal political activity. The first leads to a form of hypertrophy, one aspect of which is called "bureaucracy" in a pejorative sense and "officialdom," the other to internal friction and dissipation of energy. Both result in

excessive "overhead" and in excessive restriction of both freedom and responsibility in lower, if not in all, ranks. These
tendencies in the "organization of organization" create a philosophy of totalitarianism, which I believe to be inherent in scalar
organizations.[15] If this be a correct generalization, its validity
is largely concealed from casual observation by the fact that
nearly all scalar organizations are subordinate to the corrective
influence of superior powers — to the states — and especially of
the competition of other scalar organizations as well as of those
of free agreement. But when the scalar organization is of superior power, as it is of states, or supreme as would be true of
a genuine world scalar organization, only contrary forces of
custom, culture, philosophy, or religion, could possibly be sufficient to curb the propensity of totalitarian government.

III. TWO PROBLEMS OF STRUCTURAL BALANCE IN SCALAR ORGANIZATION

Let us assume that planners begin with a strong predilection
for a scalar organization of world government such that the
considerations hereinabove adduced give no pause to their decision. They still must plan a scalar organization not vaguely
in general outline, but in specific terms, with a substantial
degree of definition, i.e., with a constitution. It will be in point
then to call attention to two further structural problems they
must face.

For many purposes, it is convenient, though somewhat superficial, to regard individuals as the basic atoms of organization,
whether of free agreement or scalar. When individuals come
together cooperatively in organization in small groups, which

---

[15] A thorough and to me quite conclusive demonstration of this inherent
tendency is given by Robert Michels in his *Political Parties, a Sociological Study
of the Oligarchical Tendencies of Modern Democracy*, Hearst's International
Library Co., New York, 1915. His examples are chiefly from the history of
socialist parties in western Europe.

in turn become associated with other groups, these initial groups become as molecules or as primary cells of a complex organization. Now it is of importance to the problem of international and world organization to observe that in lateral organization the relative size or importance of either individuals or "cells" is not of general significance. Organization by free agreement not only can be, but perhaps most frequently is, established between individuals not of equal status, power, prestige, or capacity, or between scalar organizations of widely different size and importance. All that is essential is that they be equal with respect to the particular agreements into which they enter, *i.e.,* that they be mutual agreements. There is no necessity of formal balance between the parties forming an organization of free agreement.

The reverse is generally true of individuals or primary groups of a scalar organization viewed laterally, *i.e.,* those on the same level. In addition, a second balance between a superior cell and its subordinate cells seems required.

The simplest illustration of the first balance required may be taken from the operation of a simple scalar organization cell — say a leader and six subordinates. This organization falls short if all six subordinates do not have equal status subordinate to that of the leader. Equality of status is evidenced and maintained by two sets of relationships — an equal acceptance of orders of the leader and a dependence of the leader equally upon each, including equal dependence upon their advice.

This ideal situation is seldom approached. Usually, the equality of status of the six men fails because of the inequality of their capacities and loyalties and the differences in their motives. Moderate discrepancies will not disrupt the organization, but will merely reduce its ideal effectiveness and efficiency. But great discrepancies will lead either to adaptation of the leader's orders to and his reliance upon the lowest capacity available, seriously restricting the performance of the others with depression of their enthusiasm and loyalty, or the leader more and more gives orders to, and relies especially upon, the more able. He thereby destroys the formal equality of status, creating favoritism, destroying discipline, and overloading the more able and underdeveloping the least able individuals.[16]

This is a highly condensed and simplified summary to illustrate principles of an array of concrete cases displaying an indefinitely large variety of nuances. The principles appear to obtain also in the much more complex situations where several scalar organizations are parts of a superior scalar organization. For example, take a large industrial organization made up of four or five departmental organizations under a chief executive (and his staff). The status of the heads of these departments should be equal; otherwise the chief executive will more and more rely upon and transfer to the "superior" department the functions of others, thereby overloading it and breaking down the others, and compelling the heads of these "inferior" departments to accept the status of bystanders in the general councils. The importance of these departments may vary. When their functions are the same, but they cover different territories, inequality may be corrected by reassignment of territory. When they perform different functions, the departments may vary widely in numbers of individuals, in size and value of plants included, in cost or returns. Thus they are incommensurable. In such circumstances, equality or inequality is a matter of comparative dispensability or indispensability to the organization as a whole. Equality of status means "regarded as equally indispensable to the organization," a definition which may be used for even the simplest conditions where there is specialization of function.

When individual members of an organization or when sub-

---

[16] I believe there is sufficient basis for a useful discussion of general methods of correcting unbalance of this kind and of their limitations, but to undertake it would carry us too far afield in this paper.

ordinate groups cannot be eliminated, one of the solutions of scalar-organization unbalance is not available. With some qualifications unnecessary to recite here, this is the case with respect to national governmental organizations and their citizens; and it is the case of any world organization of which the immediately subordinate organizations would be sovereign nations highly variable in size, population, wealth, culture, potential power. Since they cannot be eliminated, equality of status sufficient for working purposes is impossible without constructing intermediate groups (regional hegemonies). The League of Nations scheme as a basis for world scalar organization would appear to be impossible. The maintenance of equal degrees of sovereignty on the basis of historical development is incompatible with the necessities of world scalar organization. It *is* compatible with lateral world organization. One price of a genuine scalar organization of the world may be not merely limitation of national sovereignties but the destruction of many of them. What planner can foresee the consequences?

A second kind of balance is also necessary between scalar-organization cells vertically regarded. The problem of attaining and maintaining this balance is as subtle as it is important. Every single subordinate in scalar organization is absolutely subordinate to the superior authority. Formally this is also true of a group of subordinates, but informally there seems to be necessary a kind of equality between the superior and the subordinate group as a whole. In healthy organizations, a superior will override the judgment of a group of subordinates at his peril and only in a crisis or emergency or where a decision must be made in some new field outside their competence. The problem is not one of potential insurrection. It is rather one of maintenance of free communication between superior and subordinate men and of a workable distribution of responsibility. This is seriously injured if judgment is overridden arbitrarily. The development of adequate support is retarded if responsibility or the sharing of it is withheld, or there is centralization of authority above the capacity of the superior. What is here stated in terms of persons is equally, or more, applicable to groups and to subgroups.

In scalar organizations, the tendency toward formal totalitarianism has the effect of destroying the balance between "layers" of organization here under discussion. Since the limited capacities of men compel in fact a delegation of responsibilities, there is inevitably a conflict between the excessive formal authority of the central control and the actual working of the organization. This conflict between principle and practice can be controlled by informal organization. This would appear to me to be the case of the Catholic Church, a highly authoritarian scalar organization, secularly viewed. The doctrines of faith universally held by its members and its common religious practice are the basis of the informal organization or communion, which I regard as maintaining the "vertical" balance.

The "divine" rights of a central world bureaucracy inherent in a world scalar organization could only be kept in balance, as I conceive, by a world informal organization similarly based upon a transcendental doctrine — if not of common religion, at least of common philosophy — say, respecting the brotherhood of man — or common belief in "natural law." [17]

V

In the preceding sections I have tried to show that planning world government or indeed much less grandiose organization is a delusory enterprise, if by "planning" one understands a blueprint or constitution of a future society which, being adopted, can substantially be accomplished. The first step was to consider the limitations of planning on a very small scale, distinguishing between planning a strategic modification of a

[17] Cf. Christopher Dawson, *The Judgment of Nations.*

single element or factor in a total situation otherwise constant, and the planning of a total system of complex interdependencies. As to the first, failure is common enough; as to the second, apparent success appears to be usually fortuitous.

The second step was to give a few examples from history of the revolutionary character of governmental systems to show how in the past unpredicted and generally unpredictable developments occurred contrary to the intention of those initiating events, and contrary to definite, well-matured plans.

The third step was to sketch in part the nature of organization for the purpose of showing what kind of materials it is that the world planner has to work with. The emphasis was upon our ignorance rather than upon our knowledge of these materials. But a few recognizable problems as to which our ignorance appears crucial, were brought to the fore. The first of these was that of developing, shaping, and guiding the informal organization of the world as the indispensable base for any stable organization. The second problem set forth was that of the choosing between lateral and scalar organization, the practicability of either depending upon an adequate and commensurate informal unity of mankind. It was emphasized that inherent in lateral organization were relative freedom, flexibility, adaptability, progressiveness, competition, friction, and combativeness; that inherent in scalar organization is lack of freedom, security, emphasis upon official status, conservatism, power, and a totalitarian orientation. Finally, a few additional problems of the maintenance of workable equilibrium in scalar organizations were touched upon.

All of this, and much more, should, I suppose, need to be treated definitely by the competent planner. I suggest that at present the honest planner could present his plan only with a long list of his basic assumptions, a series of colossal guesses which would deprive his plan of emotional support and political appeal.

My purpose has been to show that "blueprints" of future societies, even small ones, cannot be made. It seems worthwhile to do this because false notions about this subject are widespread and the public are being misled and deceived. "Plan" and "planning" are being presented as pass words to Utopia by idealists, inexperienced intellectuals, dishonest reformers, and political charlatans. Perhaps the worst effect is that this inevitably leads in the end to disparagement of genuine planning, a process of developing and applying knowledge and intelligence to our affairs. Long experience in planning has taught me that utopian blueprints are delusory, but it has also taught something of the nature and utility of effective planning. It seems likely that those without such experience often place their hope in "blueprints" through misunderstanding of planning and of its functions and limitations.

The art of planning and of using plans effectively has been much practiced, but little generalized knowledge of it has been formulated. I shall only attempt here a very rough sketch of parts of a theory of planning, chiefly in order that a false interpretation of this paper may be avoided.

First we should be concerned with what a plan is and what are its elements. I would at once emphasize the distinction between the formal or explicit plan — a drawing, a prescription, a list of specifications, a schedule, a constitution — to which the name "plan" is often applied for current convenience, and the complete true, or working, plan. The greater part of a complete plan is unexpressed thought (intention), implied or assumed action not stated, and the materials or "givens" of the situation to which it relates, much of which is also not made explicit. These are all essential parts of a plan. We should also note that a plan is not a plan until it is accepted as a basis of action. Decision "to proceed according to" is essential. Prior to acceptance it is either an ideal construction of abstract factors, or is a preliminary and tentative stage of the process of

planning, or nothing more than an expression of wishful thinking. Many a man has found what he thought a beautiful plan
defective when faced with the responsibility of adopting it.

We may now discriminate some of the elements of a plan.
The first is the purpose or the ends to be attained by the contemplated action. This is inherent in the plan, not external to
it, as seems to be often supposed. This is best shown by the
fact that frequently purposes or ends are revised or developed
in the process of planning. It is one function of planning to
determine ends as well as means. This is closely related to the
second element of a plan, its feasibility as a program of action.
Unless a plan can be executed, it is no plan. Determining
feasibility is often the major effort of the planning process.

The third element is the materials, the "givens," of the situation relevant to the plan. Without actors there can be no action, and without materials nothing to act upon. In some
kinds of plans, *e.g.*, architectural plans, much of this is explicitly stated in the formal plan, *i.e.*, drawings plus specifications. In most kinds of planning this is not so. In the conferences and debates in the process of planning, however, usually
much attention is given to the materials which are thereafter
assumed to be understood by the executors of the working plan.

The next element we may call the commitments of the
plan — the contemplated irrevocable effects of taking action in
accordance with the plan, the history to be created that will
constitute a new situation — promises, expenditures, alterations,
creative work, etc. Good planners will usually make the commitments as few as are believed consistent with the attainment
of immediate ends *and the maintenance of a position for effective further planning*. Freedom and flexibility, not rigidity,
are important desiderata of planning. "Carefully planned to
the last detail" usually makes good sense only for some kinds
of short-run action chiefly relating to physical construction.

This conservative principle will also be complemented by the next element, positive provision for uncertainties. These uncertainties are of three categories: (1) as to the past, *i.e.,* the significance of history and experience; (2) as to the present, *i.e.,* the facts of the situation and the estimate of inherent trends; and (3) as to the estimates of the future. Wise men of affairs, lawyers, physicians, politicians, and scientists are, I think, usually aware of these categories in their own fields. Habitual recognition of them seems essential to good planning.[18] In the planning of physical structures, deliberate provision is made for uncertainty through "factors of safety" and limitation of tolerance. In financial planning, reserves, surpluses, and other provisions for contingencies are used. "Checks and balances," the separation of the powers, is an analogous provision for uncertainties in political planning.

Finally, to complete this tentative list we must include the element of responsibility for decision already mentioned. An important aspect of it is courage.

So much for the elements of specific plans. If the only plans made were discrete, in a course of action for the most part unplanned, as in much personal behavior, this might be the end of the discourse. But in the larger organized endeavors and even in the personal action of some individuals, specific plans are not discrete but are interrelated steps in a series, stages in a more or less continuous process of planning. As the situation changes, estimates become facts or errors, the "givens" are altered, the purposes are revised, new commitments are made.

---

[18] A curious lacuna in the economic literature on uncertainty and risk is its failure to recognize that "knowledge" of the present is almost as speculative as estimate of the future, especially with respect to geographically widespread systems and organic or social systems. In my present work (USO), for example, it will require three months before the situation as of today can be presented statistically, and many important facts will not be comprehensively reported. I must act today on the basis of an estimate of the present situation. The doctrine of *"ex ante"* and *"ex post"* of the Swedish economists is the beginning of recognition of the point.

The chapters on this process of combining action and thought systematically could, I suspect, be written almost in the form and partly in the language of Dewey's *Logic,* for the process of inquiry to attain valid knowledge is, I take it, but a special case of the general theory of intellectually guided purposeful action.[19]

It is now in order to give some attention to the kinds of planning. I distinguish here three fundamental kinds, though perhaps there are many more, and call them: (1) strategic planning; (2) functional planning; and (3) evolutionary planning.

(1) Strategic planning involves instrumental action and what Mannheim called inventive thinking, or what I should rather state as cause-and-effect reasoning. It is planning which exemplifies in action *post hoc, ergo propter hoc,* a logical fallacy in general, but practically valid where *hoc* is some deliberate action followed by the attainment of the desired end. This is the dominant type of planning, and the reasoning which determines it is the *only type which most men as yet can use.* It predominates in the greater part of the intellectually determined behavior of practically all men.[20]

(2) Functional planning relates to the creation or maintenance of situations as wholes, not to individual things or events. It regards the distinguishable components of the system as in general inseparable, interdependent, and interacting. The prime consideration is the preservation of the system by the maintenance of equilibrium. The reasoning in this planning is noncausal. In general, the only adequate intellectual tools for functional plannings are mathematical, best exempli-

[19] John Dewey, *Logic the Theory of Inquiry,* Henry Holt and Co., New York, 1938.

[20] In connection with this and the succeeding three paragraphs consult Karl Mannheim, *Man and Society in an Age of Reconstruction,* especially Part IV, *Thought at the Level of Planning.*

fied in application to physical systems. In many systems in which planning is attempted quantitative measurements are lacking and mathematically calculated treatment of concrete problems not feasible. On the other hand, verbal language is quite inadequate for the purpose. In consequence planners have to acquire, through constant working in the system, a familiarity granting an intuitive grasp of the interdependencies involved and have largely to translate their comprehension into the inadequate and misleading cause-and-effect language of common usage. Hence, statesmen, executives, and administrators are unable to avoid misrepresenting their understanding or "sense of the situation" and often are self-contradictory. Hence, also, the emphasis upon the need of long experience to qualify men for effective behavior — and planning — in activities which superficially seem to involve no great intellectual difficulty.

Functional planning frequently involves provision for simultaneous operations or for operations in definite serial order contemplated simultaneously; but in practice it is usually necessary by trial and error to select single specific operating or strategic factors, action upon which is then planned strategically.

The gulf between strategic planning and functional planning, between cause-and-effect reasoning and interdependent thinking, is wide and constitutes one of the main problems of the development of social and political planning. In a civilization in which more and more reliance is placed on large and numerous explicit systems of interdependencies, the action of leaders becomes less and less comprehensible to those whose reasoning and experience is limited to strategic planning. This is already a most important cause of dissension and disorganization, not so much because inadequate communication and misunderstanding are involved as because conceptions of the justice or injustice of concrete acts are radically different depending upon whether the cause-and-effect or the functional approach is used. For example, a workman regards his wage as a specific effect of his productive effort. The manager fundamentally must regard that wage as a function of a wage-and-employment system, itself a function of a cooperative system, maintenance of which is essential to paying any wage or providing any productive opportunity. My experience and observation lead me to believe that we may have here a difficulty as great as differences of race, religion, and culture in the maintenance of organization.

(3) Evolutionary planning is that involving attainment of a future situation or system through a series of intermediate states or systems. It is well exemplified in the production of many chemicals, in building the new bridge while the trains still run, in replacing the wheels while the car is moving (Mannheim's illustration). It would be characteristic of important social and political planning.

I shall merely mention the dependence of planning upon personnel, upon the will to execute, upon leadership, and the effect of planning on the characters and capacities of men. The organization of planning as a specialized activity, and the interrelation of specialized planning and executive organizations also are matters that in their time need exposition.

This is sufficient to show that the rejection of the notion of "blueprinting" society or government for the future does not imply the abandonment of intelligent effort in the guidance of social evolution. It is also sufficient to suggest the long experience to be acquired before efficient planning of and in large societies could be possible. The blueprints of planning will be blueprints of details. The grand and final plan is a concept contradictory of the planning process, as if a scientist should erect a working hypothesis to the status of fundamental truth, thereby closing his mind and terminating his inquiry. Perhaps the beginning of wisdom in the application of the art of planning to organization and society is to leave a place for the cure of Hippocrates, *vis medicatrix naturae,* and to preach the virtues of sincerity and humility.

There are problems connected with rational handling of the future which are even more perplexing than those of the past. Involved in any possible planning for the future is our fundamental recognition that the only possible attitude in the face of experience is acceptance. Perhaps some of us have for a few brief seconds played with the idea that we would refuse to accept some unwelcome fact just discovered, and we may have allowed ourselves the suspicion of a thought that we might in that way *compel* the fact to take on the aspect that we so urgently desired. I am likely to feel like this when I break a test tube. But in the next moment we probably recovered ourselves in panic from such a fleeting aberration in the recognition that in that direction lies insanity.

— P. W. BRIDGMAN

APPENDIX

(Correspondence with Professor Lawrence J. Henderson concerning the defectiveness of chains of deductive reasoning and the fallacy of "other things being equal," especially in political and social fields.) [21]

The late Lawrence J. Henderson at the time of his death was Abbott and James Lawrence Professor of Chemistry in Harvard College, a Senior Fellow and chairman of the Society of Fellows at Harvard, and foreign secretary of the National Academy of Science. He was a teacher of the history of science, and a distinguished physiologist, and had for many years been a professor in the Harvard Medical School. In recent years he had become much interested in the work of the Harvard Graduate School of Business Administration, the Fatigue Laboratory of which was developed under his guidance, and in sociology. It was in connection with his latter interest that I had the good fortune to work with him and it was chiefly through his suggestion that I gave the Lowell Lectures published as *The Functions of the Executive.*

[21] Brief comment from Clarence E. Pickett is also gratefully acknowledged.

On March 16, 1939, I wrote Professor Henderson about some current matters and then made the following request:

I wish you could find the time and have the inclination to put down in writing, for my own purposes, if for no other, what you said to me about the limit of the number of steps in deductive reasoning which can be relied upon without correction for, or checking with, the facts. Your statement was a summary of what you had said at the meeting of economists in which you had the discussion with Schumpeter, and you said, I think, that you had checked the induction from your experience in respect to this matter with other scientists and mathematicians. It is a point that Dewey could well have made in writing his *Logic,* and it fits perfectly into his analysis of the process of inquiry. So far as I am concerned, it was worth the whole trip to Cambridge, and I should think it was a bit of wisdom that deserves wide currency among the intellectuals.

Professor Henderson's reply of March 20, 1939, reads in part as follows:

Dear Barnard:

What I said about steps in deductive reasoning comes to something like this: Twenty years ago when I began to deal with several variables simultaneously in my experimental work I found that I was, roughly speaking, always wrong in my expectations of how things were going to turn out. Formerly when dealing with a couple of variables, the work being quantitative, I had been not very rarely right. I think I was from the first even more interested than annoyed. At all events, after a while I began to think about the matter and gradually got clearer about the question. Then presently I read Pareto's *Sociology* for the first time and found much relevant stuff there.

It goes without saying that if you have everything neatly formulated in mathematical terms, if the terms are quite unambiguous, and if you do nothing but perform standard mathematical operations, you come out all right. That is to say, the result is in general as good as the material that you start with. But even here it is absolutely necessary to carry through the operations. As an illustration, I enclose a bit of algebra.

Equations (1), (2), and (3), being given straightforward algebraical work, give as a result the values of $x, y,$ and t as indicated. Now look at the equations (1), (2a), and (3), with a parallel solution, to the right. You will see that the only change is that (2a) has a 6 substituted for a *10.*

Now nobody but a lightning calculator or a person good at mental algebra could work out the effect of this change from *10* to *6* in one equation upon the values of x, y, and t, and if you are reasoning in words about economic, political, or social phenomena you are dealing with a situation of this kind, only immensely more complicated. It is sheer nonsense to suppose that you can reach a satisfactory conclusion without the algebraical work under such circumstances.

Now look next at the tabulation of the values of y corresponding to equation (1) alone. I have given first a table showing values that appear in the above calculations and then, secondly, a table for evenly spaced values of t and x. In both tables, for the left-hand column x and y are positively correlated, for the middle column x and y are independent, and for the right-hand column negatively correlated. This is an example of the fallacy of other things being equal or *pari passu*. If you hold other things equal, Table 2, at $T = 1$, you get one result. If you hold them equal at $T = 3$, you get the opposite result. If you hold them at $T = 2$, y is a constant, x a variable. If you think the t as time, you see how easily an error might come in. In the first table, middle compartment, top row, you have the further difficulty of the indeterminate form. All these difficulties are entirely relevant.

Now, for a more general statement, because of such difficulties and innumerable others, especially those that are analogous to using Boyle's Law, when the temperature is varying too widely, which is what Whitehead means by "misplaced concreteness," you cannot trust more than one or at most two steps in reasoning, even when reasoning is perfectly sound, at least in the range of the social sciences. In accordance with what I first said, you also cannot trust your reasoning in such circumstances. Therefore, as Bacon remarked, *Novum Organum,* Book I, Aphorism X, "The subtlety of nature is greater many times over than the subtlety of the senses and understanding," and Aphorism XXIV, "The subtlety of nature is greater many times over than the subtlety of argument."

All this may be a little disjointed, but I think the points are clear enough. If not, upbraid me and I will try to make them clearer.

Yours very sincerely,

L. J. Henderson

ALGEBRAIC ILLUSTRATION

N.B. if $y = \dfrac{x + t}{x + 2}$, $x - xy - 2y + t = 0$

(1) $x - xy - 2y + t = 0$	(1) $x - xy - 2y + t = 0$
(2) $3x + 2y + t = 10$	(2a) $3x + 2y + t = 6$
(3) $x + y = 3$	(3) $x + y = 3$
THEN:	**THEN:**
$y = 3 - x$	$y = 3 - x$
$3x + 6 - 2x + t = 10$	$3x + 6 - 2x + t = 6$
$t = 4 - x$	$t = -x$
$4 - x(3 - x) - 2(3 - x) = 0$	$x(3 - x) + 2(3 - x) = 0$
$x^2 - x = 2$	$x^2 - x = 6$
So: $x = 2, y = 1, t = 2$	So: $x = 3, y = 0, t = -3$
or: $x = -1, y = 4, t = 5$	or: $x = -2, y = 5, t = 2$

Tabulations of values of y for $y = \dfrac{x + t}{x + 2}$

TABLE 1

$t = -3$	$t = 2$	$t = 5$
$y = \dfrac{x - 3}{x + 2}$	$y = \dfrac{x + 2}{x + 2}$	$y = \dfrac{x + 5}{x + 2}$

$x =$				
-2	$-\infty$	$\dfrac{0}{0}$	$+\infty$	
-1	-4	$+1.00$	$+4$	values of y
2	-0.25	$+1.00$	$+1.75$	
3	0	$+1.00$	$+1.60$	

TABLE 2

$t = 1$	$t = 2$	$t = 3$
$y = \dfrac{x + 1}{x + 2}$	$y = \dfrac{x + 2}{x + 2}$	$y = \dfrac{x + 3}{x + 2}$

$x =$				
1	.67	1.00	1.33	
2	.75	1.00	1.25	values of y
3	.80	1.00	1.20	

A REVIEW OF BARBARA WOOTTON'S
Freedom under Planning [1]

M RS. WOOTTON'S book is written mainly to challenge and refute Professor Hayek's *Road to Serfdom*. She concerns herself chiefly with his assertions to the effect that the planning of an economy is inevitably totalitarian and destructive of freedom. Hence, a review of *Freedom under Planning* has to extend somewhat to *The Road to Serfdom*. The indictment of planning in the latter is carefully drawn, and thoroughly reasoned. It deserves challenge and competent criticism. Wootton undertakes to do a part of this task in a manner that is "earthy" and "practical." She does this with competence, breadth, good sense, temperance, and with the courage frankly and squarely to state factors that embarrass her position. Her book is useful and important.

There are many who are merely leftish, or puzzled, or who reluctantly believe "planning" inevitable, but whose fears mount as the history of fascism, nazism, and Russian communism is revealed. Wootton's book will be a boon of comfort to them. Wishful thinkers, and the timid, will not be willing to read it critically. For them it will be enough that someone of standing and competence, apparently fearing totalitarianism and not a dogmatic socialist, gives assurance that, though there is danger, we really might have planning and still not lose our freedoms, at least not many, and not the most important. But to

[1] *Freedom under Planning* by Barbara Wootton, Chapel Hill, University of North Carolina Press. The review was published in the *Southern Economic Journal*, Vol. XII, No. 3, January 1946, pp. 290 ff. Copyright 1946, by the Southern Economic Association.

the liberal, now sometimes called reactionary, who reads Wootton's book thoughtfully and critically, it seems substantially to confirm Hayek's thesis. Why this is so will be briefly shown later. To those who do not believe planning is inevitable, this will be encouraging, for they will hope that adequate attention to the warnings of Hayek will change the trend. But to others, who think planning is probably inevitable, Wootton's confirmation of Hayek will be depressing.

The question of the inevitability of planning is not discussed by Wootton, but is by Hayek in what I regard as his weakest and most vulnerable chapter, "The 'Inevitability' of Planning." The question is relevant here, because the significance of Wootton's as well as Hayek's book is much affected. For, if planning is inevitable, then the pessimist will accept it as involving serfdom; and the optimist will hope that invention, innovation, discovery of new ways of men, may avert the impending disaster. Wootton will inspire that hope.

We may infer that Wootton does regard planning as inevitable, for she says (chapter i): "If Miss Jaeger is right and *any* plan is incompatible with the chief economic, political and civil freedoms, then the problems concerned with the differences between one plan and another are not worth discussing. *We are sunk anyway*" (my emphasis). But although Wootton does not directly attack Hayek's denial of the inevitability of planning, in chapter iv she does attack the possibility Hayek regards as the true alternative, *i.e.,* a full and free competition. She says: "And to crown all, we have no reason to suppose that anything approaching this régime of perfect competition exists, or has ever existed or is likely to exist. On the contrary, all the evidence shows that we are travelling away from it." And later: "But, for technical reasons, the shape which modern industry has taken is ill-adapted to a world of genuinely open and free and universal competition." Again: "The weakness of the thorough-going critics of conscious determination of economic priorities is that they constantly compare an ideal, theoretical consumer-sovereignty (in which demand corresponds precisely to desire and all production is competitive) with the actualities of planning in a world of flesh and blood and imperfect institution." In a note to this last sentence she says: "This defect seems to me to underlie the whole thesis of books like Professor Hayek's *Road to Serfdom* . . . The alternatives are not planning or Utopia; they are planning, for better or worse, and a planless world to which very serious exception can be taken on good grounds . . ." In this, Wootton has, in my opinion, far the best of the argument. Hayek's position seems dogmatic and unrealistic.

Wootton means by "planning," the conscious determination of "economic priorities" by public authorities, with primary emphasis upon production. The protagonists of such planning assume that "objectives exist which can properly be described as for the benefit of all," and that these objectives can be ascertained with reasonable accuracy. However, Wootton asserts that "no plan can give people what they want as distinct from what somebody else thinks they want, or ought to want" and that the problem of the common good in any scientific and quantitative sense is insoluble. This may amaze and disconcert many advocates of planning. It is the basis of Wootton's position that planning is a matter of degree. The implication is that what is the proper degree depends upon how much freedom of one kind we are willing to give up to gain freedom of another kind. If *either* the extreme conservative position, as represented by Miss Jaeger (or Hayek) *or* the extreme left position, as represented by Harold Laski is right (either, Wootton says, *could* be right) then simultaneous enjoyment of economic, civil, and political freedoms is impossible. So far as this goes, Wootton shows undogmatic open-mindedness and common sense. However, it leaves open for further inquiry whether, once a system of planning is in effect, it can or will be operated by authorities consistently with some generally acceptable degree of planning. To Hayek, on the basis of history and experience and the avowed judgment of important socialists, this is impossible; Wootton counters with respect to several categories of freedoms (with two exceptions) that it *could* be done although how is not yet always demonstrable.

The first of these categories is that of cultural freedom — freedom of thought, speech, art, religion. One gets the impression that Wootton would sacrifice planning if it requires control of culture. She grants that economic planning does put the planners in a position to destroy cultural freedom. She says (chapter ii): "The problem of planning for freedom thus resolves itself into the problem of determinate planning for indeterminate cultural ends. Stated thus it sounds insoluble." But, she thinks, practically it is soluble if certain conditions are observed. She thinks "the critical point is this business of *knowing* where to stop" (my emphasis). Also: "The second condition of successful economic planning for indeterminate cultural ends is that the planners should show a nice discrimination in their methods." It seems that in this section the logic is rather confused, the terms contradictory, the thinking wishful. It is conceivable, I grant, that it is possible to plan for no cultural ends and without restricting cultural freedom, but it has not yet been done. Wootton states (chapter ii) that "the U.S.S.R. offers the one and only example of really comprehensive planning in time of peace which the world has ever seen. Throughout this experiment the degree of both civil and cultural freedom has been intolerably low" because "the Soviet plans have, however, from the beginning been avowedly devoted to promotion of specific cultural ends . . .," the very thing she says should not be done.

In this part of the argument I think Hayek wins. However, neither Wootton nor Hayek evinces more than a superficial knowledge of the sociology of organization or practical under-

standing of organization management. What Wootton neg-
lects and Hayek does not emphasize is that planners make errors, that in a régime of planning, knowledge of errors destroys
confidence, that without confidence plans are in danger of not
being executed, that change of planners may disrupt planning
and be destructive of its organization. Men may be *driven* by
the responsibilities involved, to interfere with cultural freedom where *they* think necessary because they see social chaos
if their plans are changed except as they find changes advisable
and practicable.

The second category of freedoms comprises "civil rights concerned with the method of enforcement of the law, and the
position of the actual or supposed lawbreaker," *i.e.,* trial by
jury, habeas corpus, etc. These, Wootton thinks, are least likely
to be threatened by economic planning, and says: "Even Professor Hayek does not specifically suggest that these are in danger." So she spends some time explaining why soviet history
in this respect is not probative or conclusive. But the reflective
reader, remembering also Germany, Italy, and Turkey, will
be reminded that under planning, administrative rules and decisions supersede largely both the law and the concept of civil
rights so far as concrete behavior is concerned. Even in the
United States before the war, it was increasingly true that men
were denied even the right to employment by administrative
decision; and the use of the mails is a privilege, not a right,
that may be denied at least in some circumstances by administrative decisions not appealable to the courts. As planning
increases, the area of this kind of regulation has to increase.
It may be used, as it has been, to deprive men of the right to
food or shelter or livelihood without formally abrogating any
constitutional rights.

And now we come to the economic freedoms. Wootton divides them into two groups, the freedoms of consumers and
those of producers. Each of these groups is again subdivided.

First comes freedom of choice as to immediately offered goods. The best system here is just plain money freedom: you buy what you will with the money you have. This may be qualified by a point-stamp system, described as it has been operated in Great Britain, and by rationing. But our author does so hope planning will permit simple money choice. In peace times this does not seem to be an excessive hope, at least for the richer countries.

Next comes that peculiar abstract kind of freedom known by the orthodox economists as "consumers' sovereignty." This means, I think, the effect of free choice in the market upon the relative and to a considerable extent the absolute production of various goods, of kinds both already produced and *those potentially producible*. Wootton gives a quite elaborate popular exposition of the economic theory of consumers' sovereignty. She shows that this is an exaggerated notion, because prices and corresponding costs have to be taken into account, and competition has to be really free for the theory to be good — and it isn't that kind of world anyway. If it were, the individual consumer would not know he was effecting any control of production and so would not miss the freedom of his "sovereignty" if he had none. Now the reason stated for this "somewhat abstract discussion" is that consumers' sovereignty is "one of the chief arguments used by those professional economists who are opponents of planning." In agreement with the economists Wootton plumps right out with, "You can't have consumers' sovereignty and planning." This freedom has to go; but she says this freedom is a fake and worth nothing anyway. In effect, that is, Hayek is right, but the point is not worth being right about. It is here that I think Wootton is least realistic and not quite awake. One only has to have observed what the women of Moscow would do to get shoes or stockings in the 1930's while the subway was being decorated in marble onyx and stainless steel to get the point; or to observe the force of the desire for "good will" on the actual behavior of producers. So far as she goes, I think Wootton's economic analysis is sound. It seems to me she just couldn't bear to go far enough. And so she enunciates these "classic" sentences: "It can hardly be said that people greatly prize a freedom the nature of which they do not fully understand and the absence or presence of which they would not even recognize! These last few words are important. The real reason why full consumer-sovereignty is not a matter that people trouble about is that they are generally unaware whether they have freedom or not." Similar statements could be made of the freedoms of the bill of rights, but they seem irrelevant to the issue.

Next is the freedom of the consumer to buy *when* he wants to, *i.e.,* his freedom to save. In very simplified form we now are presented with what I take to be the Keynesian doctrine. There cannot be freedom here but "happily there is every reason [sic] to *hope* [my emphasis] that this conflict between consumer liberty and producer security can be resolved: and resolved without grave interference with the consumer's liberty to spend as he pleases . . . The road out of the difficulty lies not through dictating to the consumer when he may or may not spend his money; but through the state undertaking both to make good the deficiencies, and to compensate for the vagaries, of consumer spending." She fails to discuss whether what the state does involves dictating to consumers through taxes and other interferences or indirectly by some form of arbitrary inflation or deflation.

And so we come next to chapter vi which begins the exposition with respect to producers' freedoms. The first of these is freedom of choice of employment. The suspension of such freedom in Britain during the war has taught its importance. "Choice of employment is a fundamental liberty." But we learn for the first time that the primary object of planning is full employment, defined as a condition where there are more

vacant positions than applicants to fill them. The *right to be
employed* complicates the granting of *choice* of employment as
a fundamental liberty. For it is understood that the practical
conditions of planning must recognize the need of increasing
and decreasing employment in the various productive enterprises. How, then, does the planner accomplish the shifts while
still leaving freedom to choose what one will do and where,
and in what particular job one will or will not work? How
does one deal with those unwilling to work, those unwilling to
shift, and those not willing to stay put? The answer is: by
force of either legal or economic sanctions or inducements.
Wootton places great emphasis on economic inducements to
control the distribution of labor as granting the maximum freedom, or sense of freedom, because it is less personal than the
application of legal sanctions. Her analysis of the elements of
freedom of choice of employment is admirable, and her exposition of economic incentives, especially as related to unemployment insurance and subsistence relief in Britain, is illuminating. Nevertheless, though all these words may soften,
they cannot avert the blow: either you order men to work
when and where plan requires it, or you fix economic incentives and penalties that induce them "voluntarily," as under
the non-planned system, to do the equivalent. The latter
method clearly offers the greater freedom; but to work it the
planner must control the incentives. If this degree of freedom
of choice of employment is granted it is inescapable that freedom of bargaining must be denied.

This dilemma is candidly set forth though with some rationalization and considerable embarrassment, as I read it, in
chapter vii, "Freedom of Collective Bargaining." A few quotations will suffice. "With a free choice of employment every
pattern of production implies a corresponding pattern of
wages." "It is in fact the business of a Union to be anti-social."
"Blame for the consequences of the anti-social policies of sec-

tional organizations like Trade Unions lies, not upon the societies themselves, but upon our practice of allowing issues by which many parties are affected to be settled by one or two of those parties alone." "What it means is that *all* [my emphasis] the familiar methods of adjusting wages are quite inappropriate to the demands of economic planning." "Any suggestion that wage rates should generally be fixed by public bodies immediately raises once more the question of sanctions. And here I think we have to face the fact that any conceivable sanction is *bound to do violence to deeply cherished liberties.*" (My emphasis.) "The long and the short of it is, then, that planned production implies either compulsory industrial direction or a planned wage structure." "I do not think we should underestimate the seriousness of this dilemma. The Russians have resolved it, apparently, by withholding the right of free collective bargaining as we understand this."

What more could Hayek ask than this? Well, he could say: "You have gone so far in your acceptance of planning that you do not even mention the loss of the bargaining rights of *individuals,* though you did emphasize the importance of their freedoms as consumers. Even today, this is unrealistic in Great Britain and the United States. You thereby greatly obscure the importance of the admission you make."

Wootton discusses freedom of enterprise in chapter viii. Its brevity and inadequacy seem due to underestimating its importance. This in turn is based on the view that freedom of enterprise "is of practical interest only to a small minority [sic]. For every hundred people who work in an employed capacity [presumably in Great Britain], there were, in the census of 1931, fewer than eight in business on their own account." Also "freedom of enterprise had suffered many encroachments even before the War," which seems quite irrelevant to the subject, and is really begging the question. Wootton finds the socialist-capitalist controversy "barren." "The whole question of the relation between freedom of enterprise and planning needs to be treated as a matter more of expediency than of principle." "Realistic discussion must concern itself, not with two extreme alternatives, but with the endless possible quantitative variations of mixture."

In the long chapter ix Wootton deals with her final category, the political freedoms, "the right freely to express criticism of the Government and its works; the right to form opposition political parties; the right to replace one Government and legislature by another, without resort to force." What Wootton says is that as democratic governments are *presently* organized, and with political attitudes what they *now* are, *planning is incompatible with political freedom;* and that it could be made compatible by changes in organization and political attitudes. In effect, a Pollyanna approach permits us to substitute pleasant possibilities for uncertainties and probabilities. These propositions are an exceedingly weak basis for refuting Hayek as Wootton explicitly attempts to do in this chapter.

The incompatibility of planning and political freedoms derives from the fact that planning requires continuity of administration, whereas democratic political life, as we know it, requires frequent changes. A few quotations will establish that this is Wootton's appraisal of the situation. "The dilemma that we have to resolve here is that economic planning demands continuity, and political freedom appears to imply instability. Nothing can alter the fact that we cannot both make effective long-term plans, and continually exercise the right to change our minds about anything at any time." "It follows from all this that planning and political freedom are *only* [my emphasis] compatible in so far as people are *really* of one mind about what they want to plan for; otherwise continuity could only be maintained by tying the hands of an opposition which disapproved not only of the methods, but also of the objects, of the plan." "As we have seen, planning is only possible without sacrifice of political freedom, if the limits of any plan which is to be exempt from continual disturbance fall within the boundaries of genuine agreement on the purposes which the plan is to achieve."

One possible method of solving the dilemma, which has already had some success, is the scheme of "independent" boards and government corporations. As a means of securing continuity of planning and political freedom these are open to two objections as stated by Wootton. The first is that by taking such boards and corporations out of politics "we are in fact diminishing political freedom." Although Wootton thinks she is going to answer this objection adequately later, I cannot find that she does so. This negative objection leads to the second which is on the positive side. "An independent organization inevitably develops a kind of life of its own, and, equally inevitably, it becomes a focus of vested interests: people connected with it want to keep it going for no better reason than the fact that it is there." In other words, "planning" as carried on through boards and government corporations involves government by bureaucracy, not effectively to be regulated either by competition or by detached government control. Substantially all that Wootton can say about this is: "If these objections are felt to be serious, again it cannot pass the wit of man or woman to invent alternative methods of arranging the mechanics of stability under a democratic constitution." "Cannot pass the wit of man or woman" is about the feeblest argument of the book.

But it leads to what is called the "real" question: "Is there a will? The most powerful of all criticism of long-term planning comes from those who suggest that the reason for continual changes of mind is the lack of common agreement to give shape and direction to our plans." This is the problem of political attitudes and processes. Hayek, according to Wootton, has stated "that in modern political units, no such agree-

ment is possible," and that the area of genuine agreement is
so limited that "the planner is driven to resort to improper devices for concealing disagreement, or for creating the appearance of agreement which has no real existence." "Planning"
according to Hayek, says Wootton, "thus leads to the eventual
abolition of all political, as well as of a good slice of cultural
and civil freedom." This "depressing and pessimistic doctrine
. . . presumes an utterly skeptical attitude as to the common
good." The attempt is then made to combat the "doctrine"
with much sophistry ending in the following pearl of definition: "The common good is, in fact, anything which is commonly thought to be good."

This really calls for exegesis. It gets it. "At any time the
common good consists *only* [my emphasis] of those social objectives about which there is in fact *genuine* and *general*
agreement [my emphasis]; including, it must be repeated,
agreement from those who personally cannot gain and may
lose in an individual, materialistic sense from the realization
of those objectives." Wootton tries to show that the area of
agreement is constantly increasing, despite which she also says:
"More and more, ours is a world of many little coteries, combining and recombining in complex patterns of harmony and
discord; and less and less is it a world of large groups in clear
and permanent conflict with each other." Despite the increase
(if it is) of the areas of agreement, modern democratic political
tactics involve emphasis on the disagreements. Therefore,
"some modification of this attitude will, I think, be necessary
if democratic governments are to undertake extensive economic
planning. As we have seen, planning is only possible without
sacrifice of political freedom, if the limits of any plan which
is to be exempt from continual disturbance fall within the
boundaries of genuine agreement on the purposes which the
plan is to achieve."

But how is it possible to plan if essential parts lie outside "the area of agreement"? Wootton does not answer that question, which is critical for the whole argument. Rather, she says that instead of "manufacturing" agreement (it is Hayek's word to which she makes strong objection) "it is a case of *discovering* agreement prior to action. This is the technique in which democracy is so little practiced." From all of this I would say the outlook is not very promising. Wootton virtually abandons planning: "If, however, any serious attempt at continuous planning within, *but not beyond* [my emphasis], the limits of the area of common agreement is to be made, some method must be found of determining where that area ends." And again: "What I have suggested is, on the contrary, that agreement should be *discovered;* and that, where and in so far as it obtains, so far *and no further* [my emphasis] should economic and political programs *be placed out of reach* [my emphasis] of the unstable jousts of Parliamentary democracy." But is it possible to have general planning which omits those parts which are outside the area of agreement; and how does one determine what is the area of agreement in a democracy except through the parliament? Wootton's answer is slippery and unrealistic. She has already said, as I noted early in this review, that the problem of the common good in any quantitative and scientific sense is insoluble.

This whole chapter is, to my mind, the sophistry of a wishful thinker. The strongest evidence of this, aside from critical analysis, is that twice Wootton resorts to the argument "It cannot pass the wit of man or woman" to "devise" or to "invent" solutions which in fact have not been devised or invented. "It is much *to be hoped* [my emphasis] that the attempt to explore the range of interparty agreement will lead to calmer and clearer thinking about the distinction between social ends and means; and, to a much more experimental attitude toward choice of means." This relates to another proposition: "The simple basic principle remains — the more people are agreed, the less there is left to quarrel about: and *vice versa.*" Is this true, or is it not rather that the wider the area of agreement and of common undertaking, the longer the periphery in which there is cultural diversification and disagreement?

We now come to the end. Wootton has undertaken to refute Hayek's position that planning and totalitarianism are *necessary* correlates. At least in so far as Hayek's demonstration is restricted to *The Road to Serfdom,* I think Wootton partly succeeds in this purpose. She shows that there is reasonable ground for asserting the *possibility* of a considerable degree of freedom under planning, although in doing so she rather convinces me, so far as the record goes, that Hayek is probably, though not necessarily, right.

However this may be, Wootton herself emphasizes that demonstrating a reasonable possibility of freedom under planning does not assure such freedom. Whether planning with freedom can be had depends upon (1) the choice of planners; (2) a shift of political activity from center to circumference; and (3) the quality and attitude of the people. Comment on the third factor is reserved for the concluding paragraphs. On the second it may be noted that in his *Democracy in America,* first volume, de Tocqueville emphasized the importance in the success of American democracy of wide distribution and localization of political power. Wootton is urging something only apparently similar under planning, for she has already amply demonstrated that political power, whatever the practical modes of delegation of authority, must be centralized if there is to be central planning. The critical issue is where the final decision must be located. Saying that politically apathetic people should participate in local boards having executive or judicial responsibilities does not dispose of that issue.

But this is all of secondary importance compared with the question of leaders of planning and how they will behave. Indeed, Wootton entitles this final chapter "Who Is to Plan the Planners?" "Here," she says, "all the old clichés are just as true as they ever were — power corrupts, absolute power still corrupts absolutely, and eternal vigilance is just as much the price of liberty as ever it was."

Professor Hayek stated that economic planning inevitably brings the worst to the top. He gave three specific reasons for this which Wootton spends some time in challenging. I think she really avoids his reasons to some extent; but she completely evades the more fundamental argument of Hayek's chapter "Why the Worst Get on Top" which might better have been entitled "Why Those on Top Are or Become the Worst." This is that when an organization is set up to plan an economy, *i.e.*, an authoritarian state, the ends of the state become paramount; and where a dominant party is necessary to maintain the dominance of the state, the ends of party organization are dominant over all morals of individuals. There is nothing new in this to anyone who studies either history or the sociology of organization. In every organization the distinction between "personal capacity" and "official capacity," between personal morals and impersonal or official behavior is well recognized. But in the ordinary subsidiary organizations of non-totalitarian societies the difference is not great as a rule, because by law and custom individualistic morals are regarded generally as applicable also to organizations and are to a great extent enforced against them by the state, by others acting through the courts, and by the need for maintaining good will. But when the state, as planner, is above all and determines all and all depend directly upon it, there is no one to enforce any system of morals against it, and the maintenance of its authority becomes the only fundamental rule of morals. Its failure spells social chaos and the extinction of its leaders. The most moral and amiable of leaders under these conditions must be governed by the needs of organization, just as the most amiable and tender-hearted of generals must not only slaughter the enemy but lead their own men to slaughter to do so. The organization, *i.e.,* the army, will otherwise be lost and fail of its mission. Compared with this problem, that of selection and control of leaders is minor. What Wootton has to say about it seems sentimental and immature, not to say amateur, speculation. This is enough to say of it.

The fundamental weaknesses of Wootton's book lie in its exaggerated intellectualist approach rather common among pink advocates of planning. Despite its "practical" flavor it scarcely ever suggests the problem of errors in planning, nor the fact that the planners will necessarily operate unconsciously as the agents of a "spontaneous automatism" — intellectual, emotional, and political — that is more subtle and even more hidden than the "unseen hand" of unplanned economic systems. Hayek's error seems to me to be failure to make more explicit that his argument was not mere rationalization or merely a limited amount of deduction from scanty history. Nevertheless, it does not follow that because we can see no way out none can evolve even if it cannot be planned. Without being able to defend myself against his argument, as Wootton has not, I nevertheless cannot accept as the only alternatives serfdom or perpetual revolution, *i.e.,* a wide-open and intolerable competition. Barbara Wootton has performed a valiant service in assaulting a stronghold, even though it is not, I think, an impregnable one.

If this review exhibits indefiniteness and vacillation in some respects, I should like to attribute such qualities to the eternal dilemma which the problem of freedom presents. Without touching on the philosophical question of free will and determinism, there are two fundamental questions only glanced at by either Wootton or Hayek: (1) Do people want freedom, or how much do they want it, or how much freedom can people take? (2) What is the most general condition of freedom, and how can that condition be established?

Hayek and Wootton both assume that people want freedom or ought to have it, though the question with Wootton is more one of degree than with Hayek. This question is much broader than the problem of freedom versus security or that of freedom versus equality, matters that deserve more attention than the purposes of either Hayek or Wootton permitted. The fundamental question is the desire for freedom versus reluctance toward responsibility. When tyranny reaches the point of physical restraint, injury, and murder, there is little question that freedom is desired. The instinct of self-preservation provides for that. Short of that point, however, the imposition of freedom may easily be a severe form of coercion, involving boredom, frustration, or persistent worry. Those who appear most free, in positions of high command, seek constantly to devise rules, norms, formulas, and organization by which decisions are made for them, and they are relieved of liberty of action, though not relieved of responsibility or deprived of the illusion of control. The burden of conscious deliberation of choice quickly becomes great and unbearable, the ease of responsive obedience the strongest enemy of systems of freedom. If the people's capacity for freedom is narrowly limited, then it may be conceived to be rationed among the cultural, civic, economic, or political freedoms, or to be concentrated in one category or another; but it is difficult to conceive that people can accept complete freedom in all categories simultaneously. In this I think lies the explanation of the sincere adherence of Germans, Russians, the British and Americans, to mention no others, to different and contradictory philosophies of freedom. The insistence of the Russians that their system is democratic, which seems to many Americans so stupid and insincere, is more than communist propaganda. A new description of democracy might well be that in a democracy people have to be only as free as they want to be.

The most general condition of freedom is that of order. If

there were no order in nature it is inconceivable that there could be adaptation to it. In the social world order may be based upon conditions of nature (such as geography and climate), institutions, political systems, systems of technology, inheritance and race. Actually it is unstably based upon one or another of an almost infinite number of possible combinations of all these and other elements. But the primary necessity is order, and the question of which kind of order is preferable is secondary and may even be a meaningless question in the sense that it is generally insoluble. But to be order it must be in fact accepted behavioristically, whether it is philosophically accepted or not. Hayek advocates a political and civic order based on the rule of law; but the rule of law can produce no order unless the people abide by it. Wootton is for order based on control of economic behavior. It will produce no order if the people prefer otherwise, as evidenced by black markets and evasions, no matter how they vote. At one time in western Europe order was partly based on compulsion as respects religion. With the Reformation and religious freedom, came political order based on nationalism and the separation of church and state. We cannot have freedom without order. We apparently cannot have order and all our freedoms too.

VIII

EDUCATION FOR EXECUTIVES[1]

IN considering the problem of education for executives, I shall not undertake to discuss either curriculums or pedagogical methods or their results. I prefer, instead, to limit my statement to what I think executives need, whether or not these needs may be met through formal educational means; and I restrict myself to a few points which I consider inadequately understood or much underemphasized.

We should recognize that executives have various combinations of strengths and weaknesses. To speculate about which of them are of crucial importance, outside those of moral character, does not seem to me fruitful. In fact, the test is not what qualifications a man is supposed to possess but how effectively he actually behaves. Even this in many cases will be a matter of doubt and sometimes the subject of unwise rationalization. Nevertheless, I suppose no one doubts that without education the supply of leaders of organization competent for conditions of the modern world would be wholly inadequate; and many of us suspect that if we knew better how to train men, we should be much better able than we are to cope with the social dilemmas we confront.

I shall focus my thought on executives of the future; for the changes that are going on, whether in production or in distribution, in public affairs or in education, are in the direction of a

[1] This article is the substance of a statement made at an informal meeting of faculty members of the School of Business and of the Division of the Social Sciences of the University of Chicago, August 16, 1945. It was published in the *Journal of Business of the University of Chicago*, Vol. XVIII, No. 4, October 1945, pp. 175 ff. Copyright 1945, by the University of Chicago, and reprinted by permission of The University of Chicago Press.

much closer formal integration of social activity as a whole than has heretofore obtained. In my judgment this calls for more emphasis on the topics I shall present than I would have been inclined to give them heretofore.

One further preliminary remark: It is, I suppose, obvious to everyone who thinks about it that the most that can be accomplished in education for executives before they undertake work in the world of affairs is a preliminary training and discipline, an initial orientation, and a very limited amount of knowledge. It probably will be even more true in the future than in the past that formal knowledge and cultural development must be acquired on the initiative of the individual subsequent to institutional instruction. However, in conjunction with the instruction given in educational institutions, it seems to me that it should be persistently repeated that, even as to the subjects being taught, only a beginning can be made, and that one of the most important functions thereby performed is to help the student to learn how to continue to educate himself.

I

A need of the executive of the future is for broad interests and wide imagination and understanding. Whether or not narrowness of interest has limited present-day executives in their contribution to the general society which impinges on all their immediate activities and has also thereby restricted the performance of their direct duties is a matter of opinion. At any rate, nothing can be done about them now. However, there is a narrow-mindedness associated with the concentration heretofore deemed indispensable. In the future it would seriously limit the capacity of men to serve effectively both in the major and in the intermediate executive positions of large and small organizations. The emphasis I am placing here is upon the so-called humanities and also upon science as a part of general education. It is an emphasis that applies not merely

to instruction in the schools but also to pursuits after graduation. I hope it needs no argument that persons occupying positions of leadership in the community need an understanding
of what goes on in the world and of the nature of the interests
served by and underlying its activities. Whether teaching has
in the past been appropriate to the needs has been a matter
of informed discussion by several distinguished educators and
committees of competent and responsible authorities in educational work. My own views are in close agreement with the
criticisms and suggestions made by Wallace B. Donham in his
book, *Education for Responsible Living* (Harvard University
Press, 1944). All that I need say is that in my opinion the need
for such education has not been overemphasized by Professor
Donham or others.

I fear this brief statement might appear as merely a courteous
gesture in favor of general education, pleasing to that part of
the academic world more directly concerned and consonant
with the prevailing sentiments of educated men. I wish to
demonstrate that what I have said is more than that and is not
a reflection of the moment. About twenty years ago, an associate and I, who were general officers of a large organization,
believed that we should try by some positive means to reduce
the narrowness of view and interest that we thought afflicted
too many of the men of the upper supervisory organization,
limiting their flexibility and adaptability. Most of the several
hundred men concerned were college graduates in either engineering or liberal arts but had been out of school in most
cases fifteen years or more. We decided to subject them to a
course of lectures and reading, requiring six full-time, though
not consecutive, weeks. We enlisted the aid of Joseph H.
Willits, then dean of the Wharton School, University of
Pennsylvania, to manage the course. With a single exception,
no subject was given having anything directly to do with busi-

ness. The exception was the practice and philosophy of accounting, which every educated individual should know about. Probably this method, which would need periodic repetition to accomplish its aim fully, is impracticable because it involves too much interruption of regular work. One very able executive for the same purpose once suggested that, if practicable, it would be advantageous to give such men a sabbatical year. These are not solutions, but they are evidence that the problem has been recognized as of practical importance.

II

A second need of the executive of the future is that of superior strictly intellectual capacities. This is superficially in contradiction to what I have said on other occasions and to what I shall later say here. There is no doubt in my mind that training in the more logical disciplines tends to foreclose the minds of many to the proper appreciation of human beings. Nevertheless, for executives, as well as for many others, the world of the future is one of complex technologies and intricate techniques that cannot be adequately comprehended for practical working purposes except by formal and conscious intellectual processes. To understand the formal aspects of a complex organization; to analyze formal relationships between organizations; to deal appropriately with combinations of technological, economic, financial, social, and legal elements; and to explain them to others so manifestly call for ability in making accurate distinctions, in classification, in logical reasoning and analysis, that the point requires no argument. This means that the student needs rigorous training in subjects of intellectual difficulty, thereby to provide himself with the tools and the mental habits for dealing with certain classes of important problems that can be handled effectively only by the use of such tools.

III

Rigorous training in subjects intellectually difficult and, indeed, a large part of formal education, as I have already suggested, create a strong bias in many individuals against understanding in the field of human relations. The need of such understanding is of first importance to the executive; for human relations are the essence of managerial, employee, public, and political relations; and, in most cases, these rather than science, technology, law, or finance are the central areas of the executive functions.

The need of understanding in the field of human relations would justify long discussion. I shall confine myself to three points, all of which I think are susceptible, at the initial stages at least, of treatment in educational institutions. The first I would stress is the need of inculcating an appreciation of the importance and of the inevitability of nonlogical behavior on the part of human beings. So-called intellectuals seem disposed greatly to underestimate the importance of nonlogical behavior; and many, forgetting what the psychologists make so clear, will not recognize that it is inevitable and constitutes a large part of the behavior of any human being whatsoever. This leads to an attitude of deprecation and condescension toward those not intellectually adept, at least on the verbal level. The disposition is to characterize them as stupid, dumb, and animal-like. No proper appreciation of the individual human being or of the nature of our society seems possible to those who have such an attitude. I doubt if you will question that many who are thoroughly trained in technical fields calling for highly developed intellectual equipment have this attitude. It spreads itself all too easily among well-educated people rather generally, resulting in a kind of caste identification. Among the best demonstrations of the essential point I am making was that given at great length by Pareto in his *Mind and*

Society, and I need not elaborate the point further except to repeat that the kind of bias referred to seems to me to prevent the necessary understanding of social behavior.

Next, I think an adequate understanding in the field of human relations involves instruction as to the nature of general social systems. I am aware that, in their present state, sociology, social anthropology, and social psychology, particularly as sciences as distinct from philosophic disciplines, have been subject to much criticism. I hope I may be forgiven if I say that I believe a good deal of conflicting bunk has been taught in these fields. This argues for improvement and development, not against teaching what can be taught. In the time of Newton, or even much later, a great deal of modern physics, and much that is fundamental in it, was not known, and for this reason, perhaps, a good deal of bunk was then taught in that field. Newton was a physicist, but he also was an alchemist. There is in my opinion much that is valuable to be taught about general social systems; but for the present, at least, it might well be presented to the young student not so much as science but rather as something much better than any common-sense understanding of the world he lives in can be.

My last suggestion with respect to understanding in the field of human relations is that there should be instruction about formal organizations as organic and evolving systems. I am aware that at the present time our formal knowledge, as distinct from our "know how," of such organizations is tentative and limited. The fact remains, however, that no one is an executive, as distinct from a mere leader, except in formal organizations. The fact also is that already a good deal can be taught about such specific social systems.

In this connection I should like to make clear my reason for emphasis upon formal organizations as *organic* and *evolving* social systems. It is that we persistently think about such systems in terms of mechanical, rather than biological, analogy.

Our widespread use of mechanical and electrical systems makes this convenient. It results in regarding an organization as static and fixed, like a machine, instead of something that is living, that has to grow up, and that is ever progressing or regressing with changing states of equilibrium of the human forces involved.

I wish to make sure that you understand my point and see its importance. To this end I shall relate an experience and give a hypothetical illustration that would have been appropriate on that occasion.

There is an institution known as the Conference of Science, Philosophy and Religion which has met for several days in the fall for the last five years. Papers are not read at its meetings but, having been reproduced and distributed in advance, are discussed. Its members are theologians, philosophers, scholars, and scientists, and an occasional businessman, trying to make sense to each other with respect to fundamental problems of modern society. Two years ago world organization was the central interest. Several of us had been asked to prepare papers on practical organization aspects of the problem. The discussion was arranged as a panel of the authors led by Professor Lyman Bryson. It quickly appeared that a large part of the audience was completely convinced that (1) if a good scheme of organization were worked out on paper, and (2) if men competent to fill the respective positions were recruited, then (3) we would have a working, or at least a workable, organization. I strongly protested the validity of any such idea; but my view was obviously not acceptable to those present, except for a few sociologists, historians, and jurists. Most of the audience seemed unable to believe that workable organizations cannot be created in that way. Many of you will recall the testimony of an army officer of the general staff before a congressional committee some time ago to the effect that it was feasible to train an individual to be a soldier in comparatively few weeks, but that it took much longer to create an effective division of such soldiers. That is a statement I would expect any experienced executive to accept at once.

The illustration that I thought of too late which would at least have made my point clear, if not acceptable, is as follows:

Suppose the Germans should drop a highly selective lethal gas on New Jersey that destroyed only the entire management organization of the New Jersey Bell Telephone Company (except the president, who has to be retained as a nucleus of a new organization). Now the scheme of organization of Bell Telephone companies is nearly standard. The New Jersey company is about one twentieth or one twenty-fifth of the whole system, so that, with some straining, it would in principle be feasible immediately to replace lost personnel by borrowing men from other companies. The replacing persons would know the formal organization, they would know the relations of their respective positions to all others relevant to their work, and each would possess adequate and tested technical competence for his position. How long would such an organization be able to function effectively? I would guess not more than twelve hours, especially without the sanctions of military discipline. Why? First, and most obviously, because no one would know the local conditions and how to interpret the changes in the environment to which the organization has constantly to adjust. Less obvious but much more important would be the inability of the men reliably to understand each other or to understand the employees or to be understood by them. In ordinary human relations the same words in the same context often have different meanings when uttered by different individuals. We understand people easily through our experience with them, which teaches us their special uses of words, the meaning of intonation and gestures, whether they are matter of fact or emotional, given to exaggeration or understatement, are reliable or unreliable, are reticent or voluble, and many other subtle characteristics of communication. Without the confidence that accompanies this kind of understanding, reticence, hesitation, indecision, delay, error, and panic ensue. "Know your people" is nearly as important as "know your language" in the communication upon which organized effort depends. The difficulty of communication on matters of concrete action between individuals who have not known each other is a matter of common experience, but its significance with respect to organization seems to be forgotten because the organizations we know have, in fact, developed usually through long periods. At a given time nearly everyone has habitual relationships with most of those with whom he needs to communicate regularly.

IV

The discussion of approaches to understanding human relations leads to considering the need of appreciating the importance of persuasion in human affairs. This requires emphasis because a good many people of excellent intellectual development seem to regard persuasion as something undignified or as necessarily unethical, whether it relates to the selling of useful commodities or to the inculcation of useful ideas or to changing harmful attitudes. In part, no doubt, this goes back to the failure to appreciate the importance and the inevitability of nonlogical behavior. Effective persuasion itself often involves also intrinsically nonlogical processes.

If the need of appreciating the importance of persuasion in human affairs is accepted, it leads to emphasis in education upon the development in the individual of the arts of expression, though not necessarily logical statement, in writing, oral exposition, and even public speaking, though not oratory. Certainly, one of the most important limitations, as well as one of the pre-eminently important difficulties of the modern executive, is the inability adequately in writing or in conference or in addressing substantial bodies of people to express intelligibly the facts with respect to complex situations of which he may alone have an understanding. In my estimation, society is suffering a good deal from this fact, for it is subjected to a barrage of expert verbalizers who do not know what they are talking about but are convincing to the uninformed because they talk about it very well. No one will suppose that an executive can drop other functions of management in order to become a wholesale and perennial expositor of what he is doing and why. Nevertheless, the increasing complexity of relationships will call more and more for explaining what executives are doing, or think they are doing, and more and more for a cogent justification of action in one field in its relation to other fields.

Another aspect of this subject on which I would lay emphasis is much more difficult. It will be increasingly required of the executive to translate or transform thinking on one level into that of another. The common-sense way to say this is that executives have to learn to think not only in the terms which are most convenient and appropriate from their own point of view but also in the terms of other men and from their points of view. Most people most of the time find it practically convenient to think in terms of simple cause and effect, but many of us some of the time in connection with our more complex problems have to think (often "feel" is more appropriate than "think") in terms of complex interdependencies in which no simple cause-and-effect logic is accurate or even intelligible. This calls for transformation in exposition from one type of logical process, best exemplified in mathematics, to another type which I have sometimes called "strategic reasoning." Strategic reasoning involves picking out a single factor and operating on it alone so that the effect may be said to be caused by the change in that factor. In this kind of reasoning of the everyday world the assumption is that all other things remain equal and that for all practical purposes there is only one effect.

Whether this is true or not in any particular situation can usually be found out only from experience and not by reasoning. The analogy I have found illuminating is this: Although we know that a molecule of water is composed of two atoms of hydrogen and one of oxygen, nothing that we know of the properties of either hydrogen or oxygen would suggest the properties, except weight, either physical or chemical, of water. In everyday affairs, there are innumerable situations whose characteristics are not explainable by the most thorough analysis. More and more, responsible people are dealing with the situations in which the change of one factor changes many others and there is not only potentially one effect which may be desirable but others which may be undesirable. So far as I am aware, adequate attention is not being given to the dilemma in which many executives are thereby being placed. Whatever the answer may be, the fact to which I am referring is one that can well be emphasized at an early stage in the teaching of the problems of human relations.

V

I come now to my final topic, which is the need of understanding what constitutes rational behavior toward the unknown and the unknowable. Unfortunately, not only the processes of education but habitual behavior and customary understandings persistently obscure the extent to which we live and act in a world of unknowns and of unknowables. Textbooks are written about what is known, not about what is unknown. We are overwhelmed by the enormous amount of the factual and conceptual or theoretical knowledge which is available to us, because it far exceeds the possibility of being acquired by any human being. Indeed, the propaganda for science puts all its emphasis on the known, and only rarely does a scientist in general popular discussion emphasize the unknown. Harlow Shapley, the Harvard astronomer, recently did so in a Phi Beta Kappa address which was reproduced in the *Atlantic Monthly* of August, 1945.

I believe it is desirable in teaching to give courageous emphasis to the practical fact that we often have to act without sufficient knowledge and that there is much that is literally unknowable. I am speaking now not in the philosophic sense but in the practical sense, that much knowledge, even if potentially procurable, at least cannot be obtained in time for use. I recently illustrated this from my experience as president of the United Service Organizations, where much of the information needed with respect to the activities of this far-flung organization would be at least three months old before it could reach headquarters, and much actually known was secret and could not be obtained or used. But decisions had to be made, nevertheless.

The significance of this can be more generally stated as a need for understanding the distinction between calculable and incalculable risks. A calculable risk, as I use the term, is one in which it is approximately feasible to state that out of a collection of cases or events a certain percentage will have certain characteristics without its being possible to know of which specific cases this will be so. This is true of insured risks. The principles are applicable in actual management in a good many fields for which commercial insurance is not available. Now it seems obvious that there are many risks which are in this sense quite incalculable — indeed, specifically, they may not be known or recognized. In this connection I would emphasize that the treatises I have seen on risk and uncertainty, unfortunately from the viewpoint of these remarks, proceed on the assumption that facts as to the present and the past are adequately known and that the risks and uncertainties are exclusively of the future. The point I would emphasize is that executives, though they frequently act as if to deny this, are almost always lacking in adequate knowledge as to the present conditions and are unable to recover the facts of the past in many respects. Hence, the greatest of all their risks is the appraisal of the present situation, for it is only on that appraisal that it is possible at all to construct an estimate of the uncertain future.

No doubt it is apparent to you that some men are very good and others are very poor in behavior appropriate to the uncertainties. In common parlance, some are good at not getting out on a bad limb or in not sticking out their chins when there is no need or no purpose to be served thereby. Where there cannot be adequate knowledge, there is still place for wisdom. I suspect that practical people have learned patterns of behavior that generally meet such situations and that if there can be no teaching on this subject, at least at an early stage people can be taught that this is the kind of world in which they will behave.

And, finally, in this same connection, emphasis should be placed upon the fact that most behavior of social groups is automatic or autonomic. I mean by this that what occurs is not directed from above but is the "spontaneous" result of interaction between people. What this means in practice is that people may be conditioned (by training, education, and many other methods) so that they collectively behave in what we regard as an appropriate way. When proper account is taken of this method, the executive may delegate authority with considerable confidence in areas where he could not have sufficient knowledge to permit giving specific orders, even if it were otherwise practical to issue them. This is probably the most effective of all organization methods of dealing with the relevant facts, which as a whole are unknown and, indeed, unknowable by any individual executive.

IX

FUNCTIONS AND PATHOLOGY OF STATUS
SYSTEMS IN FORMAL ORGANIZATIONS [1]

THE following is a report of a preliminary inquiry into the nature and functions of systems of status in formal organizations. So far as I am aware, this subject has not been given extensive consideration by students of organization. This neglect appears not to be due to failure to recognize the importance of problems of status in organizations but rather to failure to recognize that status is systematic, and that systems of status have a considerable degree of independence of other structural aspects of organization. Status systems are very closely related, for example, to systems of specialization, to systems of organization communication, and to systems of authority, so that differences of status have appeared to be incidental to these other structural aspects of organization and not to constitute a separate system. This view appears to be inadequate.

Formal organizations are not independent societies but are rather limited forms of social behavior growing out of the more general societies of which they are part. This observation is especially pertinent to systems of status, particularly as respects their function of providing incentives, which largely depends upon the general conception of status obtaining in society as a whole. Thus the nature of the status system in any formal organization is largely determined by the notions of class and caste governing the needs and desires of those whose behavior

---

[1] Reprinted by permission from *Industry and Society;* edited by William Foote Whyte, copyright, 1946, by the McGraw-Hill Book Company, Inc.

constitutes the formal organization. Hence, a comprehensive treatment of the subject would logically begin with the study of status in the general social system. The present inquiry is restricted to the relatively simple study of the general facts about status systems in formal organizations, and the functions that such systems serve in such organizations.

The analysis to be presented herein is based upon experience and observation of the kind commonly understood by those who have organizing and executive experience, but it does not purport to express a consensus of opinion. It sets forth that systems of status in formal organizations are necessary as a matter of need of individuals, and as imposed by the characteristics of cooperative systems, especially with respect to the techniques of communication essential to coordination. But it also appears that systems of status generate uncontrolled and even uncontrollable tendencies to rigidity, hypertrophy, and unbalance that often lead to destruction of organization.

The scheme of presentation is as follows: (I) the nature and technical apparatus of status systems; (II) the functions of status systems with respect to individuals; (III) the functions of status in cooperative systems; and (IV) the destructive tendencies of systems of status.

I. THE NATURE AND TECHNICAL APPARATUS OF SYSTEMS OF STATUS IN FORMAL ORGANIZATIONS

By "status" of an individual in an organization we mean in the present text that condition of the individual that is defined by a statement of his rights, privileges, immunities, duties, and obligations in the organization and, obversely, by a statement of the restrictions, limitations, and prohibitions governing his behavior, both determining the expectations of others in reference thereto. Status becomes systematic in an organization when appropriate recognition of assigned status becomes the duty and the practice of all participating, and when the conditions of the status of all individuals are published by means of differentiating designations, titles, appellations, insignia, or overt patterns of behavior.

Two kinds of systems of status may be discriminated, both being simultaneously observed in nearly all organizations and being partly overlapping and interdependent. The first kind, which we shall call *functional* systems of status, is that in which status does not depend upon authority and jurisdiction but upon function. The ranks are vertically divided into lateral groups of different callings, trades, crafts, métiers, divisions of labor, specializations, and professions. One common characteristic of them all is that authority of command of one over another is lacking, or is irrelevant at least to the functional status. But this does not mean that functional statuses are equally valued. On the contrary, the variation is wide, from the "low" of common, unskilled, and casual labor, intermittently attached to organizations, to the "high," *e.g.,* of the expert accountant, lawyer, architect, physician, and clergyman. Though lateral differentiation of status is not confined to formal organizations, it is a characteristic of such organizations generally and especially of the larger organizations conspicuous for their elaborate divisions of labor.

Functional status is a general attribute. For example, merely performing carpentering at a given place, which would determine specific status varying for each individual from time to time and from place to place, is not what we mean by functional status. The "carpenter" is presumed by all to have certain capacities regardless of who he is or what he is doing and conversely is presumed to have limitations, *e.g.,* he is not authorized to give medical advice. It is the presumption of capacities and limitations without necessary regard to the immediate concrete activities of the individual that is the essential feature of systematic status. The emphasis is upon the poten-

tialities of behavior, not necessarily upon the immediately observable behavior.

In the second kind of status system, which we shall call the
scalar, status is determined by (1) the relationship of superiority
or subordination in a chain of command or formal authority
and (2) by jurisdiction. In this kind of status system the primary relationships are customarily conceived as being along
vertical lines, of above and below, of superior and subordinate.
Status is distinguished by horizontal levels, and integration is
by vertical groups, several such groups exemplifying a "pyra-
mid of authority." It should be noted that status is a general
attribute of an individual associated with the occupation of a
usually rather narrowly restricted position. For example, a
naval captain possesses certain prerogatives not enjoyed by those
of inferior rank and is deemed qualified for positions for
which those of inferior rank will not ordinarily be acceptable;
but the position of command actually occupied at a given time
will be confined to a particular ship or shore station or staff
position, and the immediate authority and responsibility will
be correspondingly restricted.

Although the status systems of general societies will not be
treated in this paper, the close interrelation of general social
status and status in organizations should be noted. Where in
a general society a low status is assigned based, *e.g.,* on race,
nationality, sex, age, education, ownership of property, or
family, it is difficult in general to acquire high status in formal
organizations in that society; and where there is high social
status it tends to facilitate attainment of high organization
status, though less so in democratic than in aristocratic societies.
Conversely, those having low status in a formal organization
are not likely to have high social status, though there are many
exceptions; and those having high status, especially in important organizations, tend thereby to acquire higher general
social status. The bearing of this is that if status systems are
necessary in formal organizations, it is probable that they will

extend into general social relationships, in greater or less degree, depending upon the society.[2]

Nearly all members of formal organizations may be observed to be much preoccupied with matters of status; and the leaders or managers of such organizations are almost constantly concerned with problems of status for reasons that will be treated in some detail later. But to fix more clearly what we mean by status, it seems desirable to present briefly here the organization apparatus by which status is established and maintained. This apparatus may be described as of the following categories: (1) ceremonies of induction and appointment; (2) insignia and other public indicia of status; (3) titles and appellations of office and calling; (4) emoluments and perquisites of position and office; (5) limitations and restrictions of calling and office.

(1) The use of ceremonies of induction and appointment varies widely in different types of organizations. Ceremonial induction is common to all grades and ranks in military and religious organizations, is quite widely used in governmental and educational organizations, and is almost absent in business organizations (at least in the United States).

(2) Insignia and other indicia of status are nearly universal in military organization, especially in time of war, and in many religious organizations, especially as to the clergy. They are also used in many educational organizations on ceremonial occasions. They are little used in civil governmental organizations (except by the departments for police and fire protection) or in business organizations except for the wearing of union labor insignia in many trades and, in Europe, distinctive garb for those employed in some trades.

(3) Titles and appellations of address are universal in formal organizations both for scalar and for functional status. In the

[2] During the last several generations, when scalar organizations were developing rapidly in Germany, organization status was carried over widely into generalized status in German society, formally, *i.e.*, by title. *See* PARSONS, TALCOTT, "Democracy and Social Structure in Pre-Nazi Germany," *Journal of Legal and Political Sociology*, November, 1942.

case of functional status, the title often begins as a mere designation of the function performed, as "clerk," "bookkeeper," "lineman," "typesetter," etc., and initially has no implication of systematic status; but very quickly, since classification by functions is attended by other distinguishing conditions such as differences in compensation, such titles become also the designations of status.

(4) Emoluments, perquisites, and privileges are highly important evidences of status and are often highly valued. Care should be taken, however, to distinguish between the valuation of them as material rewards and as evidences and elements of status. They are almost universally employed in organizations of all kinds. In business and in some other organizations they are even more important than titles in fixing status. The use or nonuse of restricted quarters, automobiles, chauffeurs, private offices, private secretaries, and other perquisites in various combinations, time clocks, etc., provide a complex code that describes the system of status in effect, thoroughly understood by the initiated and fairly easily sensed by the outside observer.

(5) Both higher and lower statuses are also established and published by restrictions and limitations of behavior that relate almost exclusively to maintenance and protection of status and the status system. For example, those of higher status often cannot go to places where those of lower status are free to go, or do things that those of lower status may do, or say things, or use language, etc. Though this is well understood, these limitations are not often made explicit and they are among the most subtle elements of status systems.

This, it is hoped, is sufficient to make clear the nature and in general the technical features of systems of status in scalar organizations so far as necessary for present purposes. If so, we may proceed to the main business of studying the functions and the consequences of such systems.

II. The Functions of Systems of Status with Respect to Individuals

Systems of status of different kinds and of various degrees of elaborateness and complexity are found in most if not all formal organizations. The establishing of a nucleus of such a system is one of the very first steps in creating an organization.[3] Are these facts merely reflections of habitual attitudes and needs transferred from general society and coming down from antiquity? The view to be developed here is that systems of status, though they may be affected in degrees and in details by habitual attitudes and needs projected from the customary beliefs of people, are fundamentally determined by the necessities associated with the needs and interests of individuals as biological and social units, and upon the requirements arising from the physical and social limitations inherent in systems of cooperation. In the present section we shall deal with the relation of status systems to the needs of individuals.

It may be asserted first of all that systems of status arise from the differential needs, interests, and capacities of individuals. I shall discuss these in five topical divisions, as follows:

i. The differences in the *abilities* of individuals.

ii. The differences in the *difficulties* of doing various kinds of work.

iii. The differences in the *importance* of various kinds of work.

iv. The desire for formal status as a social or organizational tool.

v. The need for protection of the integrity of the person.

[3] In the case of corporations, corporation law provides at least often for both boards of directors and for two or more general officers. Bylaws almost always provide for additional general officers. In the case of individually owned businesses and partnerships, the nucleus of the status system rests initially directly upon property ownership. Similarly with noncommercial organizations, the first steps in organizing are likely to be to create an initial governing board and a set of officers.

I

Differences of ability with respect to any kind of effort in which there is social interest obviously lead to a recognition of difference of status of individuals in respect to that kind of effort. This does not necessarily imply superiority or inferiority in general, although, in fact, usually the lack of capacity of individuals for most kinds of effort, or even for any valued effort whatsoever, does inescapably establish for them a general position of at least technical or productive inferiority.

Differences of ability among individuals arise from a variety of conditions. The most obvious and possibly the most important are physiological or anatomical conditions, either inherent in the constitution of the individual from birth or imposed later by accident or disease. Cases of extreme physical or mental incapacity or even partial incapacity require no comment.[4] There are also some very important differences such as lethargic constitution, slowness of reactions, and lack of curiosity as contrasted with vigor, alertness, quickness of reaction, natural accuracy of physical coordination, and active curiosity. The latter characteristics or their lack when manifested in early years are especially important as affecting the capacity to receive instruction and other social conditioning and to acquire experience. Differences that are small or deemed unimportant in early years thus may cumulate to be substantial at maturity or at the end of the most active learning period.

Other differences of capacity so obviously depend upon education and specialized training that little need be said on this subject. Broadly considered, it includes the social conditioning attendant upon living in a social milieu. Differences in

---

[4] The importance of such limitations in a population is commonly disregarded. Among adults probably not less than 1 in 20, or 5 per cent, is to be so classified.

education come from differences in ability to receive instruction and from differences in interest; hence, from differences in willingness to accept the discipline and sacrifices involved; from differences in economic and social resources; and from differences in the educational resources available.

Finally, differences of individual ability arise from differences of experience. Physical, social, and intellectual skills develop through practice. There appears to be a considerable degree of chance in the distribution of opportunities for experience. There is also wide variation in the disposition to adhere to a long course of experience, to "stick to one job." Again, there is considerable variation in the capacity to learn from experience, *i.e.*, in the faculty of self-education.

Such differences among individuals as are here outlined do not prove the necessity of formal systems of status; neither, if they imply such formal systems in some respects, do they involve a formal qualification or disqualification in all respects. They do suggest that the first base upon which status systems rest is the undeniable differences, whatever their origins, between the physical, mental, and social capacities and interests of individuals. It will be recognized that these are fundamental conditions of immediate practical and inescapable significance, *e.g.*, to the teacher, the military officer, or the employer.

II

Differences in the capacities of individuals undoubtedly lead to differences of informal status quite aside from the requirements of formal organizations. For example, some groups tend to form on the basis of educational level, or physical strength, or endurance, etc. But the important significance of differences of ability stems from differences in the nature of various kinds of activities. Many kinds of work, unskilled labor, for example, usually require only sound health and normal physiological abilities. Other work, say that of a laboratory chemist, may require unusual delicacy of physiological reaction in the use of laboratory equipment, long arduous technical education, powers of imagination, thorough experience, and a willingness to work persistently without supervision or instruction. The work requires an exceptional combination of powers, some of which may need to be developed to an exceptional degree. Recognition of the status of being exceptional is forced upon such a man by his own experience. He is made aware of it by the difficulty of finding those competent to carry on his work or to assist him. He is also elevated to exceptional status by those who wish his work to be done and who find that there are few competent to do it. Those whose interests are narrowly concentrated in one field for this reason often regard exceptional ability in that field as indicating not only special but general superiority. The banker finding few who can function effectively in his field, whatever their condition of education and experience, may be led to believe that those who can do so are of status generally superior to all others. A broader view, of course, recognizes that great superiority in one field does not imply general superiority.

Thus the second base for status is, as contrasted with personal ability, the relative difficulty of things to be done. The difficulties will usually be appraised on judgment based on general experience and observation, or, more objectively, on the basis of the numbers or proportions of individuals who can or cannot do well the various tasks.

III

The exceptional ability to do things that are exceptionally difficult, while it is a sufficient basis for establishing differences of status in the general estimation, is not sufficient to establish a *system* of status involving authority or responsibility. Superiority in formal organizations depends upon exceptional ability for exceptionally difficult work of exceptional *importance.* "Importance" in this context includes more than economic importance. High status is not accorded to superior ability to do unusually difficult things of trivial character, except perhaps in very restricted circles. On the contrary, if an activity is regarded as exceptionally important, even though not very difficult, superior status is nevertheless likely to be accorded to superior ability with respect to it. This is probably most evident in the economic world, but it is readily seen in other spheres, *e.g.,* in military organization.

The importance of the work, then, establishes the importance of the position that "seeks" those of exceptional ability. Relative difficulty is a factor but is usually of minor importance except when importance is approximately equal. Status becomes systematic because activities regarded as important are systematized and organized.

IV

The next basis for status is pragmatic. Insignia and titles of status have the effect of credentials. They create a presumption with respect to the character, ability, and specific skills or functions of individuals. They are not conclusive, of course, but as preliminaries, as introductions, they save time and prevent awkwardness and embarrassment. The general's stars indicate at a glance the nature of his responsibilities and the probable relative reliability of his utterances in certain fields. The title "M.D." creates a presumption that the holder of that degree may usefully be approached without reticence about bodily ills. The degree of "Ph.D." may be granted to a fool, but very generally it is a sign of the possession of a considerable intellectual experience, scholarly or scientific skill, and mental discipline. "Vice-president" of a corporation indicates one who probably understands business language and organization. "Foreman" indicates the man through whom the most effective approach may probably be had respecting the group under him and the work they are doing. "Bishop" is the title of one whom the communicant may accept as having certain ecclesiastical responsibilities and authority and as being able to perform certain spiritual functions, though the communicant may never before have seen him or been told about him.

Generally, the possession of title and of other indicia of rank certifies that those in the best position to have responsible judgment acknowledge and publish the status indicated, which all whom it may concern may accept at least tentatively. The convenience and efficiency of the status system is such that men seek status as a necessary tool in their work; and for the same reasons it is imposed upon them by those responsible for their work. It is to be noted that this applies as much to functional status as it does to scalar status.

V

In so far as systems of status are imposed "from the top" they are expressions of the requirements of coordination rather than of the ambitions of the most able and powerful acting on the basis of personal motives. The personal motivation of most profound effect, applying equally to those of superior and to those of inferior status, is the need for protecting the integrity of the person in a social environment. This leads some to seek superior formal status, but it also leads others to refuse superior status and even to seek inferior status, depending upon the individual and the circumstances. This may be demonstrated sufficiently by presenting four modes in which the need for status is expressed: (1) the need of integrating personal history by the conferring of status; (2) the need of imputing superior status to those from whom commands are to be received; (3) the need of imputing superior status as a means of symbolizing possession of personal value in participating in an organization; and (4) the need of status as a protection against excessive claims against the individual.

(1) The need of integrating one's personal history into one's personality by the attainment of improved status and by the conferring of status publicly is exceptionally important to those who by deliberate effort or sacrifice condition themselves to the possession of superior knowledge, skill, or experience. The need is for an endorsement of the individual's past history as a creditable element in his existing personality. The granting and attainment of improved or different status here is not reward but anointment. It serves a ceremonial function of announcement, of proclamation, that an approved course has been followed by this person. Without such endorsement the effort often appears to the individual to have been in vain. A sense of frustration, sometimes devastating, may follow. Even when the individual is one of extraordinary self-sufficiency, the attainment of recognized distinction of status may be desired to maintain standing with relatives and supporting and cooperating friends. No one who watches the contemporary parade of diplomas, degrees, public honors, and the award of innumerable insignia of achievement and distinction, and who observes the reaction of individuals, of families, of organizations, and of the public to them can doubt the importance of these recognitions in nearly every field of individual and social activity. If such distinctions, often of ephemeral value, are an important element in individual behavior, it is evident that permanent position of status is even more so. It may be thought that the need of status here discussed is merely a reflection of the effect of attitudes, inculcated by mores and institutions that no doubt do reinforce the need, but the response of small children to status and the use made of status in instruction and discipline of the very young suggest that the need is more primitive and is individual.

(2) The need of imputing higher status to those from whom commands come is rather certain though it is not often obvious. It is apparent to nearly everyone on the basis of even

simple and limited experience that the coordination of effort necessary for effective cooperation can be practically secured only by specializing the function of command. It is obvious that everybody cannot give orders to everybody else at the same time and for the same activity. But except at times of great danger, to receive orders from a nondescript "some-other" is felt to be an injury to the self-respect, to the integrity, of the person. This can be avoided or alleviated only if it is felt that command is exercised by "right" either conferred by super-natural authority, or, more generally in our present society, conferred by superior ability, or by the burden of superior re-sponsibility. Men are eager to be "bossed" by superior ability, but they resent being bossed by men of no greater ability than they themselves have. So strong is this need of assigning superior status to those in positions of command that, unless the obvious facts preclude it, men will impute abilities they cannot recognize or judge. They want to believe that those of higher authority "know what they are doing" when they ap-point someone over them. Since men in the ranks are not capable of judging or are not in a position in advance to judge the competence of men in posts of command remote from them by two or more grades or even of those in immedi-ate command if special technical abilities are required (*e.g.*, the surgeon in the operating room or the navigator of a ship), this desire for the justification of subordination leads often to profuse rationalization about status and even to mythological and mystical explanations of it; but the ways in which a need is manifested ought not to be permitted to obscure its nature or the function of the means that satisfy it.

What has just been said as respects the need of imputing higher scalar status to those from whom commands are re-ceived applies somewhat less definitely and more subtly to dif-ferences in functional status where authoritative advice rather than formal authority is involved. Thus the advice or even the directions of one having the status of an expert in a particular field will be accepted against that of someone recognized as being equally expert but not having status. The subjective factor involved may be that of a diffuse feeling of public authorization to transfer responsibility to one having functional status. Though there is wide variation in the competence of those having the same status, and reliance upon mere formal status is subject to much error and abuse, nevertheless there can be little doubt that the system of functional status affords great relief to nearly everybody in practical everyday social behavior.

(3) The need felt by those of subordinate rank for imputing personal superiority to those in command, *i.e.,* the need of protecting the integrity of the person, is also expressed in sentiments of valuation of an organization as a whole. To be a member of a good organization is a personal asset. It is among the claims to distinction of most men. To be ejected from an organization is a serious, sometimes a catastrophic, injury to the integrity of the person. "Patriotism," "sense of communion," "loyalty," *"esprit de corps"* are common expressions of this attitude. Few, if any, with experience of command will doubt this, and those who observe behavior of men in military organizations in war know how powerful and indispensable this sentiment is, though perhaps not many would express the facts in terms of personal integrity.

One of the effects of this need is to sustain the system of status. For if it is not practicable for all to command, and command, *i.e.,* coordination, is essential to organization, then a system of status is indispensable. Office becomes symbolic of the organization. The commander in chief not only occupies the supreme position of command, but he speaks for the army and in his person symbolizes it.

(4) Individuals of superior ability and those of inferior ability can comfortably work together only on a basis of phys-

ical or social segregation. If no formal segregation is established, either friction and noncooperation occur or there is spontaneous informal segregation, "natural" leaders leading "natural" groups, without being adequately integrated into the system of formal command. The necessity for differentiation from the standpoint of those of inferior ability is that without it they are constantly in a position of disadvantage, under pressure to exceed their capacities, perpetually losing in a race in which no handicaps are recognized, never able to attain expected goals so long as they are treated as the equals of those who are in fact superior; therefore they are always in a position of never securing respect for what they do contribute, of always incurring disrespect for what they cannot do. Men cannot stand this kind of inferiority and its frustrations. The inferiors will group themselves and command respect by various means if they are not protected by being assigned a formal status, which, though inferior, recognizes their position as being more or less indispensable and participating, even though individually less important. The practice of labor unions of restraining the production of the more able workers of an undifferentiated craft to a level approximating that of the poorer workers, though in practice doubtless of complex motivation, seems clearly in accordance with the human needs of the situation.

Concordantly, the abler individuals press for segregation corresponding to the observed differences in abilities and in contributions. To be lumped in with inferiors in ability seems an unjust withholding of recognition, an injury to the integrity of the person. Their escape from this position will probably be more individualistic than that of those of inferior abilities who must more often resort to group solidarity. One escape, or attempt to escape, for the superior individual is to try to organize the group, to adopt a function of leadership, or to dominate without authority. Another is to leave the group for various alternative activities — found a new sect, start a new business, establish a party, and so on.

Much experience demonstrates that those who are unequal cannot work well for long as equals. But experience also demonstrates that where differences of status are recognized formally, men of very unequal abilities and importance can and do work together well for long periods.

This discussion of the relationship of integrity of the person to systems of status is not exhaustive or comprehensive, but it is enough to suggest that personal need of status system is one of their foundations.

III. The Functions of Status in Cooperative Systems

Up to this point the approach to systems of status has been in terms of the characteristics of human beings and their bearing on behavior and fundamental relationships in formal systems of cooperation. The differences in abilities arising from biological characteristics and from social conditioning and experience, the variation in the difficulties of work, the variations in importance of work, the systematic character of cooperation arising from valuation of effort, the common sense of the necessity of centralizing and specializing the function of command, the need of formalizing differences of status to protect the integrity of the socialized individual, and the symbolic functions of systems of status — all of this may be taken as the basis of the evolution of systems of status. The patterns may be as unplanned or undevised, as "spontaneous" or "instinctive" as languages. But having been evolved, they have been subjected to observation and analysis and deliberate modification, development, and design in much the same way that old languages are to some degree modified by intention and new languages have been constructed. Executives have to have a practical understanding of systems of status and are persistently occupied with concrete operations of selection, appointment, changes of status, modification of hierarchical relationships, inculcation of doctrines of command or management, and ceremonial activities, all directed to maintaining and improving the system of status and assuring that it performs its function in coordinating behavior. Much of the theory stated above appears to be sensed by executives, though not necessarily comprehended intellectually and not made explicit. The observations of practical executives would not be in terms of social psychology but in the technical terms of specific organization practice and forces.

Proceeding, then, on this level of discourse it appears necessary to the executive to recognize by some formal means differences in the ability of individuals and differences in the importance of their work or of their contribution to cooperative effort. However, executives are probably much more conscious of the necessity of systems of status as (i) a function of the system of organization communication, the fundamental process in cooperation; (ii) as an important part of the system of incentives; and (iii) as an essential means of inculcating and developing a sense of responsibility and of imposing and fixing responsibility.

I

A system of organization communication, in order that it may operate with sufficient accuracy and rapidity, has to be so designed that it may easily and quickly be assured that particular communications are (1) authentic, (2) authoritative, and (3) intelligible.

(1) Under ordinary circumstances, and especially with respect to routine matters, explicit authentication of communications is not required. Personal acquaintance with or knowledge of the communicator together with the relevance of the communication to the general context and to previous communications are sufficient. The status system is not of great

importance in this connection. But in times of emergency and great danger or in respect to important matters, explicit authentication of communications often becomes necessary. Witnessed written communications or letterheads indicating the name, position, and title of the communicator and personal introductions by mutually known third parties are among the means used. There is no doubt that here the status system greatly facilitates authentication — it is one of the practical uses of insignia of office.

(2) It is in respect to the authoritativeness of a communication, however, that we find the basic need for systems of status. The primary question of the recipient of a communication, assuming that it is authentic, *i.e.,* comes from whom it purports to come, is whether the contents of the communication may be relied upon as a basis for action. This is what we mean by authoritativeness. Authoritativeness in this context is of two kinds: functional authoritativeness; and scalar or command authoritativeness.

Whether a communication reflects the facts and needs of the situation depends upon whether the individual (or body) that emits it has the general qualifications for understanding what he (or it) communicates about and whether he is *in a position* to have the essential concrete knowledge.

A report from a carpenter about the condition of a generator in a power house is initially not credible; that of the electrician in charge is credible, though not conclusive; that of an electric power engineer is more credible and *may* be accepted as final. The authoritativeness of the report depends in part upon the qualifications of those reporting, and these are presumptively established by formal status. But a report by an electrician in Des Moines about a generator in New York is not credible. He has the qualifications in general, but he is not in a position to apply them to the situation in New York.

The purpose of the report may be to secure help in the correction of some fault. The help needed may be in the form of superior technical instruction; it may be in the form of the application of some maintenance skill or of a replacement part. The electrician is not in a position to know the status of those whose services are needed. His superior does — he knows less of the concrete situation, but he has more technical knowledge or more knowledge of the relevant status system.

The functional status system is so extraordinarily convenient in providing prima-facie evidence of the authoritativeness of communications that we depend upon it almost exclusively in the conduct of daily affairs generally as well as in all organizations. It does not imply any generalized superiority or inferiority of status in this aspect. It does not exclude discrimination as between individuals having the same status, nor does it assume errors may not occur in relying upon the prima-facie evidence granted by status. The plumber, or electrician, or lawyer, or doctor may be immature or poor or even bad, as determined by experience or surmised from observation, but even so may often be presumed to be superior to those of other statuses. A poor doctor, even though inadequate, will generally be a better advisor on medical matters than an expert plumber. Systematized functional status would seem to be absolutely indispensable for the effective operation of complex divisions of labor, and it may also be indispensable even for relatively simple divisions of labor, although in the latter condition there may be some acceptable "jacks of all trades."

(3) The special system of status associated with chains of command or hierarchy of authority depends upon each position being a "communication center," the inferior command being associated with restricted areas or fields, the higher command being more comprehensive. Outside the technical competence special to each field of organization, the general func-

tions common to all hierarchies of command are: to evaluate the meaning of communications received in the form of advices and reports, largely affected by the status of the transmitter; to know to whom communications should be relayed (*i.e.,* to know the relevant status system or "the organization"); to select that which needs to be relayed; and to translate communications, before relaying, into language appropriate to the receiver.

The system of command communication cannot effectively work except on the basis of a status system. For very small organizations communication may effectively be addressed to persons, but for larger systems status becomes primary. Contrast saying to the new office boy, "Take this order to Bill Jones in building *K*" (in which there are two Bill Joneses) and "Take this order to the foreman of section 12 in the *Y* Department in building *K*." Contrast the following orders: "Capt. Jones of Station *Y* and Capt. Smith of Station *X* will advise each other by telephone each morning as to their respective situations and will advise Major Allen of any unusual circumstances." "The Commandants of Stations *X* and *Y* will advise each other and this office each morning of their respective situations and of any unusual circumstances." In the first case any change of personalities calls for a new order — otherwise the desired collaboration will fail.

Although both functional and scalar systems of status are essential to establishing in a practicable degree the authoritativeness of communications, authoritativeness is not sufficient. Unless communications are intelligible, they cannot be acted upon correctly or effectively. Now, it is apparent that the intelligibility of a communication depends not merely upon the capacity of the communicator but also upon that of the receiver. Thus communications of the same content will differ very greatly, depending upon the status of those to whom they are addressed. Whether a communication is intelligible depends upon the use of language having the same meaning to the originator and to the receiver of the communication. This requires a selection of language, depending upon from whom and to whom the communication is made. Systems of status are an undispensable guide to the selection of appropriate language.

Thus in the power-house illustration above, if the electrician makes his report to the engineer it will be phrased differently than if made to some different official or to an outside layman. But the electrician is presumably not adept at translation to meet a wide variety of communication needs. His superior is presumably more adept.

When a communication is sent from a subordinate to his superior, it is called a report. When it is sent from the superior to the subordinate and is in peremptory terms, it is a command or order. The difference is superficial. The command implies the following report: "From my superior position I report that the situation calls for the following action on your part." Very often in fact it is in the form: The situation as known to us here is so and so; it permits you to use your own judgment, based on the local situation, i.e., issue the orders to yourself.

The executive, then, is much preoccupied with systems of status because they are important in the authentication of communications, indispensable in establishing a working presumption of the authoritativeness of their content, and essential to their intelligibility.

II

Systems of status are also important because maintenance of status and improvement of status are among the essential incentives to cooperation. The scarcity of effective incentives calls for use of many kinds of incentives; and their wise use requires, especially in larger organizations, their systematic use.

Status as an incentive has two aspects suggested earlier. The first is that of prestige for its own sake, as a reinforcement of the ego, as security for the integrity of the person. This is an important need of many individuals. They will work hard to satisfy it and forego much to attain it. The second aspect is that of prestige as a valuable or indispensable means to other ends. Thus some men endure publicity or accept conspicuous positions of onerous character as a means of supporting organizations or of eliciting the support of others because they like philanthropic, or scientific, or cultural work, which is their fundamental incentive.

The importance of status as an incentive is shown by the immense amount of work and sacrifice made by innumerable volunteer heads of social, philanthropic, religious, political, and scientific organizations. For some the motive is directly personal. For others it is the "good of the cause" and the personal incentive is satisfaction in the promotion of that cause.

These are perhaps the most obvious instances of the importance of status as incentive. The executive is frequently concerned with the instances where material rewards are by themselves ineffective and status proves to be the controlling or a necessary supplementary incentive. He is also concerned with the still less conspicuous cases where prestige is a negative incentive, where preferred status is regarded as too burdensome, and where it is believed to be a limitation on personal liberties.

III

The system of status is a strong and probably an indispensable developer of the sense of responsibility and therefore of stability and reliability. Loss of status is more than loss of its emoluments; it is more than loss of prestige. It is a serious injury to the personality. Thus while improvement of status is important, especially to the more able, and desirable to many, loss of status is much more generally resisted. It is difficult to accept, or to be accepted in, a reduced status. Indeed, the fear of losing status is what leads some to refuse advancement of status. The desire for improvement of status and especially the desire to protect status appear to be the basis of the sense of general responsibility. Responsibility is established and enforced by specific penalties for specific failures and by limitation of status or by loss of a particular status for failure in general. Although both methods in conjunction are most effective, of the two it would appear that the second is much more effective than the first, especially as to those above low levels of status. In view of the extreme importance of dependable behavior, the function of status in creating and maintaining dependable behavior is probably indispensable. The extent of criminal behavior suggests that specific sanctions are not sufficient in general to establish adequate responsibility.

We have now completed an abbreviated presentation of rationale of status systems universally found in scalar organizations. What has been set forth may well be summarized before we proceed to consider the disruptive tendencies inherent in them.

Status systems have their origins in differences in the biological and socially acquired characteristics of individuals, in differences in the difficulties of the various kinds of activities, and in differences in the valuation of these activities. Systems of status are a means of protecting the integrity of the person, especially of those of inferior ability. Superior status is often necessary to the effectiveness of the work of those of superior ability. All this is on the level of biology and social psychology. Additional observations on the level of sociology and the technique of organization show that systems of status are necessary to specialization of function; that they are essential to the system of organization communications for purposes of coordination; that they are important and sometimes indispensable as affording incentives; and that they are important in promoting the sense of responsibility and, therefore, the dependability and stability essential to cooperation. These inductions from experience and observation and from history are not scientific proof of the theory outlined; but they are believed to present a fair basis, of considerable probability of correctness, for the assertion that systems of status are not the product of irrational mores, mythologies, and rationalizations, but are specific modes of adaptation of behavior to fundamental characteristics of individuals and to the fundamental physical, biological, and social properties of systems of scalar organization.

IV. Disruptive Tendencies Inherent in Status Systems

The concern of executives is not only with the organizing functions of systems of status but with their disruptive tendencies; for, paradoxically, such systems operate like principles of growth, necessary to attain maturity, but without a self-regulative control that prevents disproportionate development of parts, unbalance, and maladaptation to the environment. Thus, the executive who promotes by positive means an improved system of status, however essential to immediate purposes, thereby generates disorganizing forces, the neutralizing of which is the more difficult in that the executive himself is a central part of the system of status. Thus the effort to detect and correct hypertrophy and abuse of the status system is somewhat akin to correcting psychopathic difficulties by introspection. Nevertheless, some executives, being individuals as well as officials, are undoubtedly able to project themselves mentally to a position outside their organizations and to view it with detachment. They then can recognize that a system of status presents a persistent dilemma.

The pathological aspects of systems of status to which these remarks refer have not been adequately investigated. We shall focus our consideration of the subject on the following topics:

I. The status system tends in time to distorted evaluation of individuals.

II. It restricts unduly the "circulation of the elite."

III. It distorts the system of distributive justice.

IV. It exaggerates administration to the detriment of leadership and morale.

V. It exalts the symbolic function beyond the level of sustainment.

VI. It limits the adaptability of an organization.

I

As set forth hereinbefore, the system of status is founded on and made necessary by the following four factors, in addition to others, relevant to the present topic: (1) differences in the abilities of individuals, (2) differences in the difficulties of various kinds of work, (3) differences in the importance of various kinds of work, and (4) the needs of the system of communication.

The first of these factors is strictly personal and individual. This does not mean, of course, that the capacities of the individual may not have been largely determined socially, but that at any given time they are the personal possession of the individual and that the application or non-application of these capacities at any given time or period is taken to be a matter of personal choice or will. To the extent that status depends upon individual ability and willingness to employ it, it may be said to be individual and not social. Personal status may to this extent be said to be correlative with personal merit. Undoubtedly, evaluation from this point of view is widely conceived as just. If this were the only basis of status, it seems probable that differences of status would be accepted as proper and necessary even where material distribution could be conceived as properly made on the basis of "to each according to need."

As we ascend to the other bases of status, more and more qualification of the conception of individual merit is required. Thus the differences in the difficulties of tasks are in some degree merely matters of the nature of the physical world and of the capacities of individuals; but where acquired skills and technologies are involved, being almost entirely of social origin, relative difficulties indirectly are socially determined. Further, almost every task in a formal society involves adaptation of behavior to and utilization of the social system itself. What is rated as easy or difficult behavior is socially evaluated. Hence, individual merit in performing the difficult often lies in capacity and willingness to resign personal preferences. The qualification on account of the social element in "difficult" is not important. "Difficult" reflects a social standard of measurement of abilities; the standard and the abilities together are a basis for status.

Variations in the *importance* of work as a basis for status are quite another matter. "Importance" is almost entirely determined socially in the same sense, though not necessarily in the same way, that economic value is determined by demand and supply as socially expressed, *i.e.,* in exchange. To the extent that the individual accepts the social valuation and does that which is regarded as important, there is personal merit. Whether the status accorded is inferior or superior, however, will depend upon whether those able and willing are relatively numerous or not. Thus, low status frequently accompanies work of primary importance in the aggregate, *e.g.,* wheat growing, in which numerous individuals are employed; high status often accompanies work which *in the aggregate* is relatively unimportant, but scarce, hence valuable, *e.g.,* silver-smithing.

The rating of the individual by the importance of his work,

a social evaluation, may be necessary to effective and efficient allocation of ability in the social system, and it may therefore be essential to the adaptation of the society as a whole to its environment. However, status so determined tends, as experience shows, to be imputed to the individual *as such* rather than to a particular socially valued *role* of the individual. When inferior status is assigned on this basis, it is transferred to the individual generally, and similarly when superior status is assigned. Thus exaggeration of personal inferiority and superiority results. The effect upon the characteristics of the individual contributors to an organization is deleterious — depressing and limiting those of inferior status, stimulating and sometimes intoxicating those of superior status. Restoring or creating morale in the one, restraining the other, then become a major problem of organization.

The system of communication by means of which coordination is secured in cooperation is a strictly social phenomenon. Being indispensable to purposeful cooperation, the necessities of the system of communication become prime, being secondary only to the prior existence of an organization whose members are willing to cooperate. Now, undoubtedly the capacity of individuals to function in a system of communications depends upon natural abilities, general knowledge and experience, facility in general and special languages, technical and other special abilities; but though often indispensable, such general capacities and potentialities are secondary to the abilities directly associated with a particular communication position and with immediate concrete knowledge. One cannot function as or in a communication center if one is not at that center nor, if at that center, without knowledge of the immediately available means of communication and of the immediately precedent communication materials, *i.e.,* what has just transpired, what further communication is called for, to whom and where further communication should be made, from whom and where communication should be elicited. Neither general nor special abilities suffice to meet the requirements if this local and concrete knowledge is not available.

Thus the primary specific abilities required in communication are those of *position* — of being at the place where communication may effectively be had and where immediate concrete knowledge may be obtained. The manning of posts of communication by those possessing the requisite abilities of position is so indispensable to cooperation that a system assuring such manning and hence of the acquirement of such abilities has precedence over all other considerations in an organization, for the breakdown of communication means immediate failure of coordination and disintegration of organization. It should not be understood from this that the general capacities and abilities of individuals are not important. If positions of communication are not manned by those of requisite general and special abilities, other than ability of position, disintegration of organization occurs slowly through failure to accomplish the aims of cooperation in ways that permit the satisfaction of the motives of the contributing individuals of an organization. The analogy is that of starvation by malnutrition as against death by trauma, such as the severing of an essential nerve. The logical as well as the instinctively acceptable choice is to avoid fatal accident even at the expense of serious and dangerous limitations; for fatal injury admits of no recovery, whereas the tendency toward dissolution even when regarded as probably certain, admits of the possibility of reversal.

It may be seen from the foregoing that schemes ensuring continuity of ordered communication are of primary importance in the adaptation of a society to its environment as well as to the attainment of ends transcending mere biological adaptation. In the past, schemes for the manning of communication posts of society have been based upon heredity (feudal systems), heredity and marriage (kinship systems), systems of property rights, systems of commission and appointment, and systems of election. All of them create differential status essential to ordered communication. The failure of any of them prior to the acceptance of a substitute system disrupts communication, and hence leads to prompt disorganization.

The indispensability of systematic communication in organization thus leads to imputing a value to the individual that relates to the role he plays and to the exaggeration of the importance of immediate local ability in communication as against more general and more personal ability.

The dilemma involved may be brought out in terms of a practical organization problem. It will ordinarily be the experience of the general executive that there are able men available for appointment to positions occupied by men recognized to be of inferior ability, but who are immediately superior with respect to local knowledge and experience in their posts and also superior in the sense that they are accepted in their posts by others. It may be clear that in the long run, provided immediate breakdown is not involved, it would be better to replace the inferior with the superior man. Nevertheless, to do so may involve costs in terms of immediate organizational disadvantages so substantial that the net effect even for the long run might be adverse. These disadvantages are: (1) If replacement is made, there will be ineptitude of functioning for a longer or shorter period. In so far as this occurs because of lack of local knowledge, it will correct itself in time, which in general will be shorter the greater the general ability of the replacing individual. The less difference there is in ability, the more doubtful is the utility of change. (2) Communication involves mutual relationships and habitual responsive reactions. A new man, entirely aside from his intrinsic abilities in the position, is new to others in the immediate communication network. *Their* capacity to function is disturbed by change.

(3) The operation of the system depends in considerable degree upon mutual confidence of the communicators. Change decreases this confidence. This is ordinarily not important as related to single changes not frequently occurring. Its importance increases at an accelerating pace as either the number or the frequency of replacements increases.

II

Thus, although systems of status are based upon individual abilities and propensities as related to tasks socially evaluated and upon the requirements of the system of communication in organizations, we find that the rating of the individual by the role he occupies and emphasis upon the importance to the organization of immediate local abilities of position lead to under- and overvaluation of individuals artificially, *i.e.,* in terms of status as an end instead of as an intermediate means.

Whatever the system or principle by which posts of communication are filled, in general, errors occur, with the result that some men of inferior abilities are placed in relatively superior positions. Moreover, even if men at a given time were all placed with ideal correctness, they change so that some become inferior to their positions, and others become more than adequate for them. Further, changes in the conditions or the purposes of cooperation may make obsolete the capacities of individuals in particular positions for which they were initially well adapted. Finally, individuals will develop or mature whose abilities are superior to those of persons who have preferred status, even though the latter have not changed and at the time of selection were the best available. The effects of aging, of physical, moral, and intellectual deterioration, of changing conditions and purposes, all call for continual readjustment and replacement in the status system. The process of readjustment and replacement is well known as the "circulation of the elite." Ideally the circulation of the elite should be so free that the status of all should at any given time be in accordance with their relative capacities and the importance of their functions. It is rather obvious that failure of this circulation to the extent that generally those of inferior capacity occupy positions of superior status will so reduce the efficiency of cooperation that survival of organization is doubtful, and that the dangers of rebellion and revolution will be so great that even for the short run such a stoppage of circulation may be fatal.

Nevertheless, even a rough approach to the ideal condition of free circulation is not possible. This is due to three essential factors: (1) A considerable degree of stability of status is necessary if improvement of status is to serve as an incentive. The more uncertain the retention of achieved status is, the fewer to whom the achievement of status will appeal. (2) The resistance to loss of status is in general stronger than desire to achieve higher status, so that it is often probable that the disruptive effects of demotion made to attain a more perfect assignment of capacities more than offset the advantages. (3) Good communication depends to a great extent upon accuracy of interpretation largely associated with habitual personal relationships. These are broken down if changes are frequent.

III

Without a system of status, as has already been stated, injustice results to those who are the less capable, by failure to protect them against overburden. If an adequate system of status is employed, it may involve injustice when the higher emoluments of higher status are greater than warranted in the sense that they are greater than necessary. It is not intended to discuss here the problem of distributive justice generally involved in differential emoluments. We shall assume that a differential system is necessary and just. What concerns us now is the distortions of justice arising from the restrictions upon freedom of promotion and demotion. The injustices arising are of two sorts: (1) The aggregate of emoluments of higher status are excessive in the sense that they do not secure the degree of service that the capacities ideally available make possible. The "social dividend" in the broadest sense is less than it should be, and the failure is a loss to those of inferior status generally. (2) Individuals capable of filling positions of higher status better than those occupying such positions are unjustly deprived of the emoluments that they are often encouraged to seek. I am using emoluments in a most general sense, including not only remuneration, but also recognition, prestige, the satisfaction of exercising one's abilities, and, for those of philanthropic motivation, the satisfactions of the largest service of which they are capable.

These injustices inherent in the practical operations of systems of status are not hidden. Men are aware of them in general and sometimes exaggerate them; and they are also aware of them specifically as affecting them individually in many circumstances. The effect of the sense of injustice involved depends partly upon the degree to which the status system is sluggish or congealed. When status is fixed by birth or limited by race or religion the extreme of disorganization may follow. When the status of individuals corresponds well with their abilities some loss of *esprit de corps* and of cooperative efficiency only may be involved.

Nevertheless, the effects of the injustices inherent in status systems are sufficiently great to require positive balancing considerations and sentiments. The consideration of most importance is that, except as to those of the lowest status (and at least in some conditions probably also to them), conservatism is protective of individuals. Even though the retention of someone in a position of higher status may be felt to be specifically unjust to one of lower status, the situation may be duplicated with respect to the latter and someone of still lower status. In some degree, recognition of a right to retain status is therefore felt to be generally just even though in particular cases the effect may be thought not so.

The sentiments supporting conservatism with respect to status are developed and maintained by rationalizations, ceremonies, and symbolism. They have for their broad purpose the inculcation of the doctrine that the primary interest of the individual is dependent upon the maintenance of the whole organization and its effective operation as a whole, and that whatever is necessary to this end, even though it adversely affects the individual, is offset even to him by the larger advantage accruing from it.

IV

An effective system of communications requires not only the stable filling of specific positions of different status, but also habitual practices and technical procedures. Failure to follow these procedures with routine persistence in general leads to confusion, lack of coordination, and inefficiency or breakdown of the system. The lines of communication, the system of status, and the associated procedures, though by no means constituting "administration," are essential tools of administration and are the most "visible" general parts of it. Being the tangible machinery of administration and indispensable to it, the protection both of status and of procedure comes to be viewed quite sincerely as the *sine qua non* of the organization.

The overvaluation of the apparatus of communication and administration is opposed to leadership and the development of leaders. It opposes leadership whose function is to promote appropriate adjustment of ends and means to new environmental conditions, because it opposes change either of status in general or of established procedures and habitual routine. This overvaluation also discourages the development of leaders by retarding the progress of the abler men and by putting an excessive premium on routine qualities.

V

Among the phenomena connected with the status system are symbols of office or of class or trade. In many cases these are not conspicuous, and may be only evident in matters of behavior, such as deference; in others, *e.g.,* military organizations, they are conspicuous. The investment of office with symbols is, moreover, often preceded by ceremonies of graduation, promotion, consecration, induction, installation, and inauguration, in which the organization and its purpose are dramatized and glorified by symbolic means. Much of this symbolic practice related to office in the abstract is transferred to the person of the individual filling the office, and in this way the individual himself by reason of his status becomes a symbol of the organization and of its purposes. This is so true that although it is usually not difficult to distinguish between personal and official acts *per se,* it is not acceptable in general to distinguish personal and official behavior of officials or for them to tolerate contumelious behavior of others toward them when wearing insignia of office or otherwise publicly known to hold office. Thus the rule is general that the private conduct of officials at least in public must not be "unbecoming a gentleman," though the rule is expressed in different manners and enforced in different degrees and in different ways. Conversely, an insult to an officer or person of other status publicly known as an officer or member of an organization is regarded as an injury to the organization itself, and especially so when committed by a member of the same organization.

This is rather evident and commonplace as respects clergymen, military personnel (in uniform), officers of the law, and judges when in courts. It is less obvious but nonetheless real in business, academic, and many other organizations where the symbols of office and status are primarily utilitarian, such as large office quarters, automobiles, guarded privacy, and special privileges.

One effect of the symbolic function of office and its associated status is to retard the circulation of the elite. The removal of an official to whom symbolic attributes have become attached, whether for incompetence or for other more reprehensible causes, unless they are very grave and publicly known, is widely felt to be derogatory to the office and to be an injury to the organization both internally and often externally as respects its prestige. Thus in one city some years ago it was said that it was practically impossible to discharge the presidents of banks except for flagrant, publicly known derelictions. Also it is often, not without ground, suspected that men are "kicked upstairs" to avoid the effects of crass degradation; and usually care and decorum are used. These considerations also in some cases explain and justify the provisions of pensions for officers under compulsory retirement rules.

Thus it comes about that the symbolism involved in office and status in the aggregate outruns the capacities of the men who have become symbols of organization.

VI

From what has been presented it is perhaps evident that in sum the effect of the status system, though essential to coherence, coordination, and *esprit de corps,* is to reduce flexibility and adaptability. When the external conditions to which an organization must be adapted are stable, the importance of flexibility and adaptability is much less than under rapidly changing conditions, and the importance of coherence and refinement of coordination, in terms of efficiency, is much greater. Were it possible to forecast for a long period what the conditions will be, the problem in principle would be merely to establish an optimum system of status, a mean between extremes minimizing disadvantages and dangers, but reasonably conserving the advantages and certainly adequate to the minimum necessities. It would hardly be appropriate to call such a problem a dilemma. The dilemma lies in the fact that future conditions cannot be forecast correctly. Hence for current purposes it is necessary to employ and often to elaborate a system of status whose inherent tendency is to become unbalanced, rigid, and unjust.

We have seen that both functional and scalar systems of status are necessary to formal organizations of scalar type, but that interests are generated by or within them forcing them to rigidity, lack of correspondence to real merits and real needs, and to hypertrophy, especially in their symbolic functions. As these matters are reflected on and as the technical apparatus of organization is studied, no doubt corrective measures can be known. They can be applied, however, only with great difficulty from within an organization, for even the chief executive is the chief of the status system and dependent on it. It therefore requires endless persistence, extraordinary ability, and great moral courage to control the dangerous developments in them. Probably, the principal needs can be summarized as three: to ensure that there is correspondence between status and ability by free movement; to prevent the systems of status from being ends or even primary means; and to see that the emoluments of office and of trade or profession are proportionate to the necessary level of incentives and morale. Some devices, e.g., retirement rules, are known that facilitate these controls; but this is not the place to discuss them.

In so far as we are concerned only with subordinate organizations, the correction of the pathologies of status systems in relatively "free" societies is largely accomplished by competition, regulation, and the pressure of public opinion, attended by the disintegration of organizations that cannot correct conditions. This does not usually involve catastrophic effects except for a few individuals, or sometimes for small communities. When the organization is that of a highly centralized state, however, it is doubtful whether there is as yet any means of correcting extreme investment of interests in the system of status, except by revolution or by military defeat.